A YOUNG PEOPLE'S
HISTORY
*of the* UNITED STATES

VOLUME ONE

# A YOUNG PEOPLE'S HISTORY of the UNITED STATES

## VOLUME ONE

### COLUMBUS *to the* SPANISH-AMERICAN WAR

# HOWARD ZINN

*Adapted by*
## REBECCA STEFOFF

**7** SEVEN STORIES PRESS
New York · Toronto · London · Melbourne

A YOUNG PEOPLE'S HISTORY OF THE UNITED STATES
VOLUME I: COLUMBUS TO THE SPANISH-AMERICAN WAR

# Howard Zinn
Adapted by Rebecca Stefoff

## SEVEN STORIES PRESS
New York • Toronto • London • Melbourne

Copyright © 2007 by Howard Zinn

*A Seven Stories Press First Edition*

SEVEN STORIES PRESS
140 Watts Street, New York, NY 10013
www.sevenstories.com

*In Canada*
Publishers Group Canada
559 College Street, Suite 402, Toronto, ON M6G 1A9

*In the UK*
Turnaround Publisher Services Ltd.
Unit 3, Olympia Trading Estate, Coburg Road, Wood Green
London N22 6TZ

*In Australia*
Palgrave Macmillan
627 Chapel Street, South Yarra, VIC 3141

College professors may order examination copies of
Seven Stories Press titles for a free six-month trial period.
To order, visit http://www.sevenstories.com/textbook
or send a fax on school letterhead to (212) 226-1411.

**Library of Congress Cataloging-in-Publication Data**
Stefoff, Rebecca, 1951-
A young people's history of the United States / Howard Zinn ; adapted by
Rebecca Stefoff.—Seven Stories Press 1st ed.
p. cm.
Includes bibliographical references and index.
ISBN-13: 978-1-58322-759-6 (paper over board : alk. paper)
ISBN-10: 1-58322-759-8 (paper over board : alk. paper)
ISBN-13: 978-1-58322-760-2 (paper over board : alk. paper)
ISBN-10: 1-58322-760-1 (paper over board : alk. paper)
1. United States—History—Juvenile literature.
I. Zinn, Howard, 1922- Young people's history of the United States. II. Title.
E178.3.S735 2007
973—dc22
2007008703

Design by Pollen, New York
Printed in the United States of America

1 2 3 4 5 6 7 8 9

# Contents

*To all the parents and teachers over the years who have asked for a people's history for young people, and to the younger generation, who we hope will use their talents to make a better world.*

❖

Thanks to Dan Simon, of Seven Stories Press, for initiating this *Young People's History* and to Theresa Noll of Seven Stories Press, for steering the project so carefully through its various stages.

❖

A special appreciation to Rebecca Stefoff, who undertook the heroic job of adapting *A People's History* for young readers.

# Introduction

EVER SINCE my book *A People's History of the United States* was published twenty-five years ago, parents and teachers have been asking me about an edition that would be attractive to youngsters. So I am very pleased that Seven Stories Press and Rebecca Stefoff have undertaken the heroic job of adapting my book for younger readers.

Over the years, some people have asked me: "Do you think that your history, which is radically different than the usual histories of the United States, is suitable for young people? Won't it create disillusionment with our country? Is it right to be so critical of the government's policies? Is it right to take down the traditional heroes of the nation, like Christopher Columbus, Andrew Jackson, Theodore Roosevelt? Isn't it unpatriotic to emphasize slavery and racism, the massacres of Indians, the exploitation of working people, the ruthless expansion of the United States at the expense of the Indians and people in other countries?

I wonder why some people think it is all right for adults to hear such a radical, critical point of view, but not teenagers or sub-teenagers? Do they think that young people are not able to deal with such matters? It seems to me it is wrong to treat young readers as if they are not mature enough to look at their nation's policies honestly. Yes, it's a matter of being honest. Just as we must, as individuals, be honest about our own failures in order to correct them, it seems to me we must do the same when evaluating our national policies.

Patriotism, in my view, does not mean unquestioning acceptance of whatever the government does. To go along with whatever your government does is not a characteristic of democracy. I remember in my own early education we were taught that it was a sign of a totalitarian state, of a dictatorship, when people did not question what their government did. If you live in a democratic state, it means you have the right to criticize your government's policies.

The basic principles of democracy are laid out in the Declaration of Independence, which was adopted in 1776 to explain why the colonies were no longer willing to accept British rule. The Declaration makes it clear that governments are not holy, not beyond criticism, because they are artificial creations, set up by the people to protect the equal right of everyone to "life, liberty, and the pursuit of happiness." And when governments do not fulfill this obligation, the Declaration says that "it is the right of the people to alter or abolish the government."

And, if it is the right of the people to "alter or abolish" the government, then surely it is their right to criticize it.

I am not worried about disillusioning young people by pointing to the flaws in the traditional heroes. We should be able to tell the truth about people whom we have been taught to look upon as heroes, but who really don't deserve that admiration. Why should we think it heroic to do as Columbus did, arrive in this hemisphere and carry on a rampage of violence, in order to find gold? Why should we think it heroic for Andrew Jackson to drive Indians out of their land? Why should we think of Theodore Roosevelt as a hero because he fought in the Spanish-American War, driving Spain out of Cuba, but also paving the way for the United States to take control of Cuba?

Yes, we all need heroes, people to admire, to see as examples of how human beings should live. But I prefer to see Bartolomé de Las Casas as a hero, for exposing Columbus's violent behavior against the Indians he encountered in the Bahamas. I prefer to see the Cherokee Indians as heroes, for resisting their removal from the lands on which they lived. To me, it is Mark Twain who is a hero, because he denounced President Theodore Roosevelt after Roosevelt had praised an American general who had massacred hundreds of people in the Philippines. I consider Helen Keller a hero because she protested against President Woodrow Wilson's decision to send young Americans into the slaughterhouse of the First World War.

My point of view, which is critical of war, racism, and economic injustice, carries over to the situation we face in the United States today.

More than five years have elapsed since the most recent edition of *A People's History*, and this young people's edition gives me an opportunity, in the final chapter of Volume Two, to bring the story up to date, to the end of 2006, halfway through the second administration of George W. Bush, and three and a half years after the start of the U.S. invasion of Iraq.

# CHAPTER ONE

# COLUMBUS
# AND THE INDIANS

ARAWAK MEN AND WOMEN CAME OUT OF
their villages onto the beaches. Full of wonder,
they swam out to get a closer look at the strange
big boat. When Christopher Columbus and his
soldiers came ashore, carrying swords, the
Arawaks ran to greet them. Columbus later wrote
about the Indians in his ship's log:

> They . . . brought us parrots and balls of cotton and spears
> and many other things, which they exchanged for the glass
> beads and hawks' bells. They willingly traded everything
> they owned. . . . They were well-built, with good bodies and
> handsome features. . . . They do not bear arms, and do not
> know them, for I showed them a sword, they took it by the
> edge and cut themselves out of ignorance. They had no
> iron. Their spears are made of cane. . . . They would make
> fine servants. . . . With fifty men we could subjugate [over-
> power] them and make them do whatever we want.

(left, detail)
Captain Mason's attack
on the Pequots'
fortified village, 1637.

I

The Arawaks lived in the Bahama Islands. Like
Indians on the American mainland, they believed
in hospitality and in sharing. But Columbus, the
first messenger to the Americas from the civilization of western Europe, was hungry for money. As
soon as he arrived in the islands, he seized some
Arawaks by force so that he could get information
from them. The information that Columbus wanted
was this: Where is the gold?

Columbus had talked the king and queen of
Spain into paying for his expedition. Like other
European states, Spain wanted gold. There was
gold in the Indies, as the people of Europe
called India and southeastern Asia. The Indies
had other valuable goods, too, such as silks and
spices. But traveling by land from Europe to
Asia was a long and dangerous journey, so the
nations of Europe were searching for a way to
reach the Indies by sea. Spain decided to gamble
on Columbus. In return for bringing back gold
and spices, Columbus would get 10 percent of
the profits. He would be made governor of any
newly discovered lands, and he would win the
title Admiral of the Ocean Sea. He set out with
three ships, hoping to become the first

European to reach Asia by sailing across the Atlantic Ocean.

Like other informed people of his time, Columbus knew that the world was round. This meant that he could sail west from Europe to reach the east. The world Columbus imagined, however, was small. He would never have made it to Asia, which was thousands of miles farther away than he thought. But he was lucky. One-fourth of the way there he came upon an unknown land between Europe and Asia.

Thirty-three days after leaving waters known to Europeans, Columbus and his men saw branches floating in the water and flocks of birds in the air. These were signs of land. Then, on October 12, 1492, a sailor called Rodrigo saw the moon shining on white sands, and cried out. It was an island in the Bahamas, in the Caribbean Sea. The first man to sight land was supposed to get a large reward, but Rodrigo never got it. Columbus claimed that he had seen a light the evening before. He got the reward.

## The Arawaks' Impossible Task

THE ARAWAK INDIANS who greeted Columbus lived in villages and practiced agriculture. Unlike the Europeans, they had no horses or other work animals, and they had no iron. What they did have was tiny gold ornaments in their ears.

Those little ornaments shaped history. Because of them, Columbus started his relationship with the Indians by taking prisoners, thinking that they could lead him to the source of the gold. He sailed to several other Caribbean islands, including Hispaniola, an island now divided between two countries, Haiti and the Dominican Republic. After one of Columbus's ships ran aground, he used wood from the wreck to build a fort in Haiti. Then he sailed back to Spain with news of his discovery, leaving thirty-nine crewmen at the fort. Their orders were to find and store the gold.

The report Columbus made to the royal Spanish court was part fact, part fiction. He claimed to have reached Asia, and he called the Arawaks "Indians," meaning people of the Indies. The islands Columbus had visited must be off the coast of China, he said. They were full of riches:

(*left*)
Bartolomé de Las Casas, 1791.

Hispaniola is a miracle. Mountains and hills, plains and pastures, are both fertile and beautiful . . . the harbors are unbelievably good and there are many wide rivers of which the majority contain gold. . . . There are many spices, and great mines of gold and other metals. . .

If the king and queen would give him just a little more help, Columbus said, he would make another voyage. This time he would come back to Spain with "as much gold as they need . . . and as many slaves as they ask."

Columbus's promises won him seventeen ships and more than 1,200 men for his second expedition. The aim was clear: slaves and gold. They went from island to island in the Caribbean, capturing Indians. But as word spread among the Indians, the Spaniards found more and more empty villages. When they got to Haiti, they found that the sailors left behind at the fort were dead. The sailors had roamed the island in gangs looking for gold, taking women and children as slaves, until the Indians had killed them in a battle.

Columbus's men searched Haiti for gold, with no success. They had to fill up the ships returning to Spain with something, so in 1495 they went on a great slave raid. Afterward, they picked five hundred captives to send to Spain. Two hundred of the Indians died on the voyage. The rest arrived alive in Spain and were put up for sale by a local church official. Columbus, who was full of religious talk, later wrote, "Let us in the name of the Holy Trinity go on sending all the slaves that can be sold."

But too many slaves died in captivity. Columbus was desperate to show a profit on his voyages. He had to make good on his promises to fill the ships with gold. In a part of Haiti where Columbus and his men imagined there was much gold, they ordered everyone over the age of thirteen to collect gold for them. Indians who did not give gold to the Spaniards had their hands cut off and bled to death.

The Indians had been given an impossible task. The only gold around was bits of gold dust in streams. So they ran away. The Spaniards hunted them down with dogs and killed them. When they took prisoners, they hanged them or burned them to death. Unable to fight against the Spanish soldiers' guns, swords, armor, and horses, the Arawaks began to commit mass suicide with poison. When the Spanish search for gold began, there were a quarter of a million Indians on Haiti.

In two years, through murder or suicide, half them were dead.

When it was clear that there was no gold left, the Indians became slaves on the Spaniards' huge estates. They were overworked and mistreated, and they died by the thousands. By 1550, only five hundred Indians remained. A century later, no Arawaks were left on the island.

## Telling Columbus's Story

WE KNOW WHAT HAPPENED ON THE Caribbean islands after Columbus came because of Bartolomé de Las Casas. He was a young priest who helped the Spanish conquer Cuba. For a while he owned a plantation where Indian slaves worked. But then Las Casas gave up his plantation and spoke out against Spanish cruelty.

Las Casas made a copy of Columbus's journal, and he also wrote a book called *History of the Indies*. In this book, he described the Indians' society and their customs. He also told how the

Spaniards treated the Indians:

> As for the newly born, they died early because their
> mothers, overworked and famished [starving], had no
> milk to nurse them, and for this reason, while I was in
> Cuba, 7,000 children died in three months. Some
> mothers even drowned their babies from sheer desper-
> ation. . . . In this way, husbands died in the mines,
> wives died at work, and children died from lack of
> milk. . . . My eyes have seen these acts so foreign to
> human nature, and now I tremble as I write. . . .

This was the start of the history of Europeans
in the Americas. It was a history of conquest, slavery, and death. But for a long time, the history
books given to children in the United States told a
different story—a tale of heroic adventure, not
bloodshed. The way the story is taught to young
people is just beginning to change.

The story of Columbus and the Indians shows
us something about how history gets written. One
of the most famous historians to write about
Columbus was Samuel Eliot Morison. He even
sailed across the Atlantic Ocean himself, retracing
Columbus's route. In 1954 Morison published a
popular book called *Christopher Columbus, Mariner.*
He said that cruel treatment by Columbus and the

Europeans who came after him caused the "complete genocide" of the Indians. *Genocide* is a harsh word. It is the name of a terrible crime—the deliberate killing of an entire ethnic or cultural group.

Morison did not lie about Columbus. He did not leave out the mass murder. But he mentioned the truth quickly and then went on to other things. By burying the fact of genocide in a lot of other information, he seemed to be saying that the mass murder wasn't very important in the big picture. By making genocide seem like a small part of the story, he took away its power to make us think differently about Columbus. At the end of the book, Morison summed up his idea of Columbus as a great man. Columbus's most important quality, Morison said, was his seamanship.

A historian must pick and choose among facts, deciding which ones to put into his or her work, which ones to leave out, and which ones to place at the center of the story. Every historian's own ideas and beliefs go into the way he or she writes history. In turn, the way history is written can shape the ideas and beliefs of the people who read it. A view of history like Morison's, a picture of the past that sees Columbus and others like him as great sailors and discoverers, but says almost nothing about their genocide, can make it seem as though what they did was right.

People who write and read history have gotten used to seeing terrible things such as conquest and murder as the price of progress. This is because many of them think that history is the story of governments, conquerors, and leaders. In this way of looking at the past, history is what happens to states, or nations. The actors in history are kings, presidents, and generals. But what about factory workers, farmers, people of color, women, and children? They make history, too.

The story of any country includes fierce conflicts between conquerors and the conquered, masters and slaves, people with power and those without power. Writing history is always a matter of taking sides. For example, I choose to tell the story of the discovery of America from the point of view of the Arawaks. I will tell the story of the U.S. Constitution from the point of view of the slaves, and the story of the Civil War from the point of view of the Irish in New York City.

I believe that history can help us imagine new possibilities for the future. One way it can do this

is by letting us see the hidden parts of the past, the times when people showed that they could resist the powerful, or join together. Maybe our future can be found in the past's moments of kindness and courage rather than its centuries of warfare. That is my approach to the history of the United States, which started with the meeting between Columbus and the Arawaks.

## More Meetings, More Fighting

The tragedy of Columbus and the Arawaks happened over and over again. Spanish conquerors Hernan Cortés and Francisco Pizarro destroyed the Aztecs of Mexico and the Incas of South America. When English settlers reached Virginia and Massachusetts, they did the same thing to the Indians they met.

Jamestown, Virginia, was the first permanent English settlement in the Americas. It was built inside a territory governed by an Indian chief named Powhatan. He watched the English settle

*(left)*
Captain Mason's attack on the Pequots' fortified village, 1637.

on his land but did not attack. In 1607, Powhatan spoke to John Smith, one of the leaders at Jamestown. The statement that has come down to us may not truly be Powhatan's words, but it sounds a lot like what other Indians said and wrote at later times. We can read Powhatan's statement as the spirit of what he thought as he watched the white men enter his territory:

> I know the difference between peace and war better than any man in my country. Why will you take by force what you may have quietly by love? Why will you destroy us who supply you with food? What can you get by war? Why are you jealous of us? We are unarmed, and willing to give you what you ask, if you come in a friendly manner, and not so simple as not to know that it is much better to eat good meat, sleep comfortably, live quietly with my wives and children, laugh and be merry with the English, and trade for their copper and hatchets, than to run away from them, and to lie cold in the woods, and feed on acorns, roots, and such trash, and be so hunted that I can neither eat nor sleep.

In the winter of 1609–1610, the English at Jamestown went through a terrible food shortage they called the "starving time." They roamed the woods looking for nuts and berries, and they dug up graves to eat the corpses. Out of five hundred colonists, all but sixty died.

Some of the colonists ran off to join the Indians, where they would at least be fed. The next summer, the governor of the colony asked Powhatan to send them back. When he refused, the colonists destroyed an Indian settlement. They kidnapped the queen of the tribe, threw her children into the water and shot them, and then stabbed her.

Twelve years later, the Indians tried to get rid of the growing English settlements. They massacred 347 men, women, and children. From then on it was total war. The English could not enslave the Indians, and they were not able to live with them, so they decided to wipe them out.

To the north, the Pilgrims settled in New England. Like the Jamestown colonists, they came to Indian land. The Pequot tribe lived in southern Connecticut and Rhode Island. The colonists wanted this land, so the war with the Pequots began. Massacres took place on both sides. The English used a form of warfare that Cortés had used in Mexico. To fill the enemy with terror, they attacked civilians, people who were not warriors.

They set fire to wigwams, and as the Indians ran out to escape the flames, the English cut them to bits with their swords.

When Columbus came to the Americas, 10 million Indians lived north of what is now Mexico. After the Europeans began settling that land, the number of Indians fell until, in time, fewer than a million remained. Many Indians died from diseases brought by the whites.

Who were these Indians? Who were the people who came out onto the beaches with presents for Columbus and his crew and who peered out of the forests at the first white settlers of Virginia and Massachusetts?

As many as 75 million Indians lived throughout the Americas before Columbus. They had hundreds of different tribal cultures and about two thousand languages. Many tribes were nomads, wanderers who lived by hunting and gathering food. Others, however, were expert farmers and lived in settled communities. Among the Iroquois, the most powerful of the northeastern tribes, land did not belong to individuals. It belonged to the entire community. People shared the work of farming and hunting, and they also shared food. Women were important and respected in Iroquois society, and the sexes shared power. Children were taught to be independent. Not only the Iroquois but other Indian tribes behaved in similar ways.

So Columbus and the Europeans who followed him did not come to an empty wilderness. They came to a world that was, in some places, as crowded as Europe. The Indians had their own history, laws, and poetry. They lived in greater equality than people in Europe did. Was "progress" enough of a reason to wipe out their societies? The fate of the Indians reminds us to look at history as something more than just a story of conquerors and leaders.

NEGROES
FOR SALE
AT AUCTION
TH'S DAY
AT 1 O'CLOCK

# CHAPTER TWO

# BLACK AND WHITE

IN THE HISTORY OF THE WORLD, THERE IS
no country where racism has been more important
than in the United States. How did this racism
start? How might it end? Another way of asking the
question might be: Can blacks and whites live
together without hatred?

Maybe history can help answer these questions. If so, the history of slavery in North
America could hold some clues, because we can
trace the coming of the first white people and the
first black people to this continent.

In North America, slavery became the normal
relation of blacks to whites. At the same time,
whites came to believe that blacks were not their
equals. For 350 years, blacks would hold a lesser
position in American society because of racism,

*(left, detail)*
A slave auction
in Virginia, 1861.

which combines ideas about black inferiority with the unequal treatment of black people.

## Why Turn to Slavery?

EVERYTHING THAT HAPPENED TO THE FIRST white settlers pushed them toward the enslavement of blacks. In Virginia, the settlers who had survived the "starving time" of 1609–1610 were joined by new arrivals. They were desperate for labor to grow enough food to stay alive. But they wanted to grow more than corn. The Virginia settlers had learned from the Indians how to grow tobacco, and in 1617 they sent the first cargo to England. The tobacco brought a high price. Even though some people thought smoking was sinful, the planters were not going to let such thoughts get in the way of making a profit. They would supply England with tobacco.

But who would do the hard work of growing the tobacco and preparing it for sale? The settlers couldn't force the Indians to work for them. The

Indians outnumbered the settlers. Even though the settlers could kill Indians with their guns, other Indians would massacre settlers in return. The settlers couldn't capture Indians and make them into slaves, either. The Indians were tough and defiant. And while the North American woods seemed strange and hostile to the settlers, the Indians were at home there. They could avoid the settlers—or escape from them.

Maybe the Virginians were angry that they couldn't control the Indians. Maybe they envied the way the Indians could take care of themselves better than the whites did, even though the whites thought that they themselves were civilized and that the Indians were savages. In his book *American Slavery, American Freedom,* historian Edmund Morgan imagines how the colonists felt about their failure to live better than the Indians, or to control them:

> The Indians, keeping to themselves, laughed at your supe-
> rior methods and lived from the land more abundantly
> and with less labor than you did. . . . And when your own
> people starting deserting in order to live with them, it was
> too much. . . . So you killed the Indians, tortured them,
> burned their villages, burned their cornfields. . . . But you
> still did not grow much corn.

Maybe those feelings of envy and anger made the settlers especially ready to become the masters of slaves. It seemed natural to the Virginians to import blacks as slave labor. After all, other colonies in the Americas were already doing it.

By 1619, a million blacks had been brought from Africa to work as slaves in the mines and sugar plantations of the Portuguese and Spanish colonies in South America and the Caribbean islands. Even earlier, fifty years before Columbus, the slave trade started when ten Africans were taken to Portugal and sold. So that in 1619, when the first twenty blacks were brought by force to Jamestown and sold to settlers, white people had been thinking of Africans as slave labor for a long time.

The Africans' helplessness made enslavement easier. The Indians were on their own land. The whites were in a new continent, but they had brought their English culture with them. But the blacks had been torn from their land and their culture. They were forced into a situation where their heritage—languages, clothes, customs, and family life—was wiped out bit by bit. Only with amazing strength of will could blacks hold on to pieces of this heritage.

Was African culture easy to destroy because it was inferior to European culture? In its own way, African civilization was as advanced as that of Europe. It was a civilization of 100 million people. They built large cities, they used iron tools, and they were skilled at farming, weaving, pottery making, and sculpture. Europeans who traveled in Africa in the sixteenth century were impressed with the kingdoms of Timbuktu and Mali. These African states were stable and organized, at a time when European states were just beginning to develop into modern nations.

Slavery existed in Africa, and Europeans sometimes pointed to that fact to excuse their own slave trade. But although slaves in Africa had a harsh life, they also had rights that those brought to America did not have. American slavery was the most cruel form of slavery in history because of two things. First, American slavery was driven by a frenzy for limitless profit. Second, it was based on racial hatred, a view that saw whites as masters and blacks as slaves. For these reasons, American slavery treated slaves as less than human.

The inhuman treatment began in Africa, where captured slaves were chained together and

(*overleaf*)
A Slave Auction in Virginia, 1861.

forced to walk to the coast, sometimes for a thousand miles. For every five blacks captured, two died during these death marches. When the survivors reached the coast they were kept in cages until they were sold.

Then they were packed aboard the slave ships, chained together in the dark, in spaces not much bigger than coffins. Some died for lack of air in the crowded, dirty cargo holds of the ships. Others jumped overboard to end their suffering. As many as a third of all the Africans shipped overseas may have died during the journey. But the trade was profitable, so merchants crammed the blacks into the holds of the slave ships like fish.

At first, the Dutch were the main slave traders. Later the English led the trade. Some Americans in New England entered the business, too. In 1637 the first American slave ship sailed from Massachusetts. Its holds were divided into racks two feet wide and six feet long, with leg irons to hold the prisoners in place.

By 1800, somewhere between 10 million and 15 million black Africans had been brought to the Americas. In all, Africa may have lost as many as 50 million human beings to death and slavery

(*left*)
African captives leaping off a slave ship off the coast of Africa, 1700s.

during the centuries that we call the beginnings of modern civilization.

Slavery got started in the American colonies because the Jamestown settlers were desperate for labor. They couldn't use Indians, and it would have been hard to use whites. But blacks were available in growing numbers, thanks to profit-seeking dealers in human flesh. And the terrible treatment Africans suffered after being captured left many of them in a state of helplessness. All of these things led to the enslavement of the blacks.

### Fear and Racism

WERE ALL BLACKS SLAVES? MAYBE THE SETTLERS considered some blacks to be servants, not slaves. The settlers had white servants, too. Would they have treated white servants differently from black ones?

A case from colonial Virginia shows that whites and blacks received very different treatment. In 1640, six white servants and one black started to run away. They were caught. The black man, named Emanuel in the court record, received thirty blows with a whip. He was also branded on one cheek and sentenced to work in shackles for a year or longer. The whites received lighter sentences.

This unequal treatment was racism, which showed itself in feelings and in actions. The whites felt superior to the blacks, and they looked at blacks with contempt. They also treated the blacks more harshly and oppressively than they treated each other. Was this racism "natural"? Did the whites dislike and mistreat the blacks because of some instinct born into them? Or was racism the result of certain conditions that can be removed?

One way to answer those questions is to find out whether any whites in the American colonies viewed blacks as their equals. And evidence shows that they did. At times when whites and blacks found themselves sharing the same problems and the same work, with the same master as their enemy, they treated each other as equals.

We don't have to talk about "natural" racial dislike to explain why slavery became established on the plantations of the American colonies. The need for labor is enough of a reason. The number of whites who came to the colonies was just not enough to meet the needs of the plantations, so the settlers turned to slaves to meet those needs. And the needs kept rising. In 1700, Virginia had six thousand slaves, one-twelfth of the colony's population. By 1763, there were 170,000 slaves, about half the population.

From the beginning, black men and women resisted their enslavement. Through resistance, they showed their dignity as human beings, if only to themselves and their brothers and sisters. Often they used methods that were hard to identify and punish, such as working slowly or secretly destroying white property. Another form of resistance was running away. Slaves freshly arrived from Africa, still holding on to the heritage of village life, would run away in groups and try to set up communities in the wilderness. Enslaved people born in America were more likely to run off alone and try to pass as free.

Runaway slaves risked pain and death. If they were caught even planning to escape, they could be punished in terrible ways. Slaves were burned, mutilated, and killed. Whites believed that severe punishments were needed to keep other slaves from becoming rebellious.

White settlers were terrified of organized black uprisings. Fear of slave revolts, it seems, was a fact of plantation life. A Virginia planter named William Byrd wrote in 1736 that if a bold slave leader arose, "a man of desperate fortune," he might start a war that would "tinge our rivers wide as they are with blood."

Such rebellions did take place—not many, but enough to create constant fear among the planters. In 1720 a settler in South Carolina wrote to London about a planned slave uprising that had been caught just in time:

> I am now to acquaint you that very lately we have had a very wicked and barbarous plot of the . . . negroes rising with a designe to destroy all the white people in the country and then to take Charles Town . . . but it pleased God it was discovered and many of them taken prisoners and some burnt and some hang'd and some banish'd.

We know of about 250 cases in which ten or more slaves joined in a revolt or plot. But not all rebellions involved slaves alone. From time to time, whites were involved in the slave resistance. As early as 1663, white servants and black slaves in Virginia formed a conspiracy to rebel and gain their freedom. The plot was betrayed and ended with executions.

In 1741, New York had ten thousand white and two thousand black slaves. After a hard winter brought much misery to poor people of both races, mysterious fires broke out. Blacks and whites were accused of conspiring together. The trial was full of high emotion and wild claims. Some people made confessions under force. Eventually two white men and two white women were executed, eighteen slaves were hanged, and thirteen slaves were burned alive.

Only one fear in the American colonies was greater than the fear of black rebellion. That was the fear that whites who were unhappy with the state of things might join with blacks to overthrow the social order. Especially in the early years of slavery, before racism was well established, some white servants were treated as badly as slaves. There was a chance that the two groups might work together.

To keep that from happening, the leaders of the colonies took steps. They gave a few new rights and benefits to poor whites. For example, in 1705 Virginia passed a law that said that masters had to give white servants some money and corn when their term of service ended. Newly freed servants would also receive some land. This made white people of the servant class less unhappy with their place in society—and less likely to side with the black slaves against the white masters.

A web of historical threads trapped blacks in American slavery. These threads were the desperation of the starving settlers, the helplessness of Africans torn from their homeland, the high profits available to slave traders and tobacco growers, and the laws and customs that allowed masters to punish rebellious slaves. Finally, to keep whites and blacks from joining together as equals, the leaders of the colonies gave poor whites small benefits and gifts of status.

The threads of this web are not "natural." They are historical, created by special circumstances. This does not mean that they would be easy to untangle. But it does mean that there is a possibility for blacks and whites to live together in a different way, under different historical circumstances.

# CHAPTER THREE

# WHO WERE THE COLONISTS?

A HUNDRED YEARS BEFORE THE AMERICAN Revolution, a rebellion broke out in Virginia. Angry colonists set Jamestown, their capital, on fire. The governor fled the burning town, and England shipped a thousand soldiers across the Atlantic, hoping to keep control of the forty thousand colonists.

This was Bacon's Rebellion. It was not a war of American colonists against the British. Instead, Bacon's Rebellion was an uprising of angry, poor colonists against two groups they saw as their enemies. One was the Indians. The other was the colonists' own rich and privileged leaders.

Bacon's Rebellion brought together groups from the lower classes. White frontiersmen started the uprising because they were angry

(*left*)
Nathaniel Bacon and his followers burning Jamestown, Virginia, 1676.

about the way the colony was being run. Then white servants and black slaves joined the rebellion. They were angry, too—mostly about the huge gap between rich and poor in Virginia.

## Nathaniel Bacon and the Rebellion

BACON'S REBELLION STARTED WITH TROUBLE on Virginia's western frontier. By the 1670s rich landowners controlled most of eastern Virginia. As a result, many ordinary people felt that they were pushed toward the frontier. Life was more dangerous there. The settlers had problems with Native Americans. They wanted the colony's leaders to fight the Indians, but the politicians and big landowners who ran the colony wouldn't fight— maybe because they were using some of the Indians as spies and allies against the others.

The frontiersmen felt that the colonial government had let them down. They were angry, and they weren't the only ones. Times were hard. Many Virginians scraped out a living in poverty or worked as servants in terrible conditions. In 1676, these unhappy Virginians found a leader in Nathaniel Bacon.

A British government report explained how Bacon appealed to his followers:

> He seduced the Vulgar and most ignorant people to believe . . . that their whole hearts and hopes were now set on Bacon. Next he charges the Governour as negligent [neglectful] and wicked, treacherous and incapable, the Lawes and Taxes as unjust and oppressive. . . .

Bacon owned a good bit of land. He probably cared more about fighting Indians than about helping the poor. Still, the common people of Virginia felt that he was on their side. They elected Bacon to the colonial government, called the House of Burgesses. Bacon was ready to send armed militias, or armed groups of citizens, to fight the Indians. These militias would act outside government control. This alarmed William Berkeley, the governor of the colony. Berkeley called Bacon a rebel and had him captured.

After two thousand of Bacon's supporters marched into Jamestown, the governor let Bacon go, in return for an apology. But as soon as Bacon was free, he gathered his militia and began raiding the Indians. The rebellion was under way.

Bacon gave his reasons for the rebellion in a paper called "Declaration of the People." It blended the frontiersmen's hatred of the Indians with the common people's anger toward the rich. Bacon accused the Berkeley government of wrongdoing, including unfair taxes and not protecting the western farmers from the Indians.

A few months later, Bacon fell sick and died at the age of twenty-nine. The rebellion didn't last long after that. A ship armed with thirty guns cruised the York River, one of the main waterways of the colony, to restore order. Its captain, Thomas Grantham, used force and tricks to disarm the last rebel bands. At the rebellion's main stronghold, Grantham found four hundred armed whites and blacks— freemen, servants, and slaves. He promised to pardon them and to free the servants and slaves. Instead, he turned his boat's guns on the rebels and took their weapons. Then he returned the servants and slaves to their masters. Eventually, twenty-three rebel leaders were hanged.

Bacon's Rebellion came about because of a chain of oppression in Virginia. The Indians had their lands seized by white frontiersmen. The frontiersmen were taxed and controlled by the rich upper classes in Jamestown. And the whole colony, rich and poor, was being used by England. The colonists grew tobacco to sell to England, but the English set the price. Each year, the king of England made a large profit from the Virginia colony.

Most people in Virginia had supported the rebellion. One member of Governor Berkeley's council said that the rebels wanted to take the colony out of the king's hands and into their own. Another said that the Indian problem was the original cause of Bacon's Rebellion, but that poor people had joined because they wanted to seize and share the wealth of the rich. Who were these rebels?

## The Underclass

THE SERVANTS WHO JOINED BACON'S Rebellion were part of a large underclass of miserably poor whites. They came to the North American colonies from English and European cities whose governments wanted to get rid of them. In England, for example, changes in land laws had driven many farmers into poverty and homelessness in the cities. New laws were passed to punish the poor, imprison them in workhouses, or send them out of the country. So some of the poor were forced to leave their homes for America. Others were drawn to America by hope—or by promises and lies about the good lives they would have there.

Many poor people bound for America became indentured servants. They signed an agreement called an indenture that said that they would repay the cost of their journey to America by working for a master for five or seven years. Often they were imprisoned after signing the indenture, so that they couldn't run away before their ship sailed.

The voyage to America from England or Europe lasted from eight to twelve weeks. If the weather was bad, the trip could take even longer, and passengers could run out of food. Poor people crossing the ocean to work as servants in the American colonies were crammed into crowded, dirty quarters. Not all of them survived the journey. Gottlieb Mittelberger, a musician who sailed

from Germany to America around 1750, wrote
about the terrible trip:

> During the journey the ship is full of pitiful signs of
> distress—smells, fumes, horrors, vomiting, various
> kinds of sea-sickness, fever, dysentery, headaches, heat,
> constipation, boils, scurvy, cancer, mouth-rot. . . . Add
> to that shortage of food, hunger, thirst, frost, heat,
> dampness, fear, misery, vexation, and lamentation as
> well as other troubles. . . . On board our ship, on a
> day on which we had a great storm, a woman about to
> give birth and unable to deliver under the circum-
> stances, was pushed through one of the portholes into
> the sea. . . .

Once they arrived in America, indentured servants were bought and sold like slaves. On March
28, 1771, the *Virginia Gazette* reported: "Just arrived
. . . the Ship Justitia, with about one Hundred
Healthy Servants, Men Women & Boys. . . . The
Sale will commence on Tuesday the 2nd of April."

More than half the colonists who came to
North America came as servants. They were
mostly English in the seventeenth century, Irish
and German in the eighteenth century. Many of
them found that life in the American colonies was
worse than they had imagined.

Beatings and whippings were common. Servant women were raped. Masters had other means of control. Strangers had to show papers to prove that they were freemen, not runaway servants. The colonial governments agreed among themselves that servants who escaped from one colony to another must be returned. (This later became part of the U.S. Constitution.)

Masters lived in fear of servants' rebellions. After Bacon's Rebellion, English soldiers stayed in Virginia to guard against future trouble. One report at the time said, "Virginia is at present poor and more populous than ever." The writer added that many people were afraid of an uprising by servants who needed basic necessities, such as clothes.

Escape was easier than rebellion. Historian Richard Morris, who wrote a book called *Government and Labor in Early America*, studied colonial newspapers and found many reports of white servants running away, sometimes in groups. Other servants went on strike and refused to work. In 1663, a Maryland master complained to the court that his servants would not do "their ordinary labor." The servants said that they were too weak to work, because the master fed them only beans and bread. The court ordered the servants to receive thirty lashes with a whip.

More and more, as servants ran away or finished their indentures, slaves replaced them. What happened to the servants after they became free? Cheerful stories tell of former servants who rose to wealth, owned land, and became important people. But in his book *Colonists in Bondage*, historian Abbot Smith reported that almost none of the wealthy, important men in the colonies had been indentured servants, and only a few of them were descended from servants.

## Rich and Poor

CLASS LINES HARDENED DURING THE colonial period. The difference between rich and poor grew sharper. At the very beginning of the Massachusetts Bay Colony, in 1630, Governor John Winthrop showed the thinking of colonial

(*detail*)
Nathaniel Bacon
and his followers
burning Jamestown,
Virginia, 1676.

leaders when he said that "in all times some must be rich, some poore." The leaders of the colonies were men of money and status. They wanted society in North America to mirror England, where a small number of people controlled the best land and much of the wealth.

The colonies grew fast in the eighteenth century. Between 1700 and 1760, their population rose from one-quarter of a million people to more than a million and a half. Agriculture, shipping, and trading grew. Small factories developed. Boston, New York, Philadelphia, and Charleston doubled and tripled in size.

Through all that growth, the upper class got most of the benefit and held most of the political power. For example, in Boston in 1770, the top 1 percent of property owners had 44 percent of the wealth.

Rich colonial merchants built mansions. People of the upper classes had their portraits painted and traveled in coaches or in chairs carried by servants or slaves. Meanwhile, the poor struggled to stay alive, to keep from freezing in cold weather. And their numbers kept rising. By the 1730s, people demanded institutions to hold the "many Beggarly people daily suffered to wander about the Streets."

The cities built poorhouses for old people, widows, cripples, and orphans, and also for unemployed people and new immigrants. The poorhouses quickly became overcrowded. A Philadelphia citizen wrote in 1748, "It is remarkable what an increase of the number of Beggars there is about town this winter." Nine years later, Boston officials spoke of "a great number of Poor" who found it hard to feed their families.

Traditional histories of the colonies make it seem that the colonists were united in the struggle against England, their outside enemy. But there was much conflict within the colonies. Slave and free, servant and master, tenant and landlord, poor and rich—disorder broke out along these lines of tension.

In 1713, Boston suffered a severe food shortage. In spite of the city's hunger, a wealthy merchant named Andrew Belcher shipped grain to the Caribbean islands, because the profit was greater there. A mob of two hundred people rioted, broke into Belcher's warehouses looking for food, and shot the lieutenant governor of the colony when he tried to stop them. Later, another Boston mob beat up the sheriff and surrounded the governor's house to protest impressment, or forced service in the navy. In 1747, poor Bostonians felt that Thomas Hutchinson, a rich merchant and official, had discriminated against them. His house mysteriously burned, while a crowd watched and cheered.

In New Jersey in the 1740s and 1750s, poor farmers clashed with rich landowners. Both groups claimed they owned the land, and the farmers rioted when the landowners demanded rent. During this time, England fought several wars that brought wealth to a few colonial shipbuilders and merchants. But to the mass of colonists, England's wars brought high taxes, unemployment, and poverty—and more anger against the rich and powerful.

## How to Rule

BY THE 1760S, THE WEALTHY ELITE that controlled the British colonies in North America had three big fears: Indian hostility, the danger of slave revolts, and the growing class anger of poor whites. What if these three groups should join together?

Bacon's Rebellion had shown the colonial leaders that it was risky to ignore the Indians, because that infuriated the white people living near the frontier. Better to make war on the Indians and gain the support of the whites. By turning the poor against the Indians, authorities might head off possible class conflict between poor and rich.

Could blacks join the Indians against the whites? This was a real threat. In the Carolinas in the 1750s, twenty-five thousand whites were outnumbered by forty thousand black slaves and sixty thousand Native Americans. Authorities decided to turn blacks and Indians against each other. They bribed Indians to return runaway slaves, and they also made it illegal for free blacks to travel in Indian country. Indian villages did shelter hundreds of runaway slaves, but blacks and Indians never united on a large scale.

The greatest fear of wealthy southern planters was that black slaves and poor whites would combine in another uprising like Bacon's

Rebellion. One tool to keep blacks and whites from uniting was racism. Edmund Morgan, a historian of slavery in Virginia, wrote in his *American Slavery, American Freedom* that racism was not a "natural" feeling about the differences between black and white. Instead, white leaders encouraged a negative view of blacks. If poor whites felt contempt for African Americans, they were less likely to join with them in rebellion.

As the colonies grew, the ruling class found another way of keeping control. Along with the very rich and the very poor, a white middle class was developing. It was made up of small planters, independent farmers, and craft workers in cities and towns. If these middle-class colonists joined forces with the merchants and big planters, they would be a solid buffer against the frontier Indians, the black slaves, and the poor whites.

The upper classes had to win the loyalty of the middle class. This meant that they had to give the middle class something, but how could they do this without damaging their own wealth or power? In the 1760s and 1770s, the ruling group found a wonderfully useful tool. That tool was the language of liberty and equality. It could unite just enough whites to fight a revolution against England—without ending slavery or inequality.

# CHAPTER FOUR

# TYRANNY IS TYRANNY

AROUND 1776, SOME IMPORTANT PEOPLE
in the British colonies of North America made a
discovery. They found that by creating a nation
and a symbol called the United States, they could
take over land, wealth, and political power from
other people who had been ruling the colonies for
Great Britain.

When we look at the American Revolution this
way, it was a work of genius. The Founding
Fathers created a new system of national control
that has worked very well for more than two hundred years.

Control was desperately needed. The colonies
boiled with discontent. By 1760 there had been
eighteen uprisings aimed at overthrowing the government of one or more colonies. There were also

(*left*)
Bonfire at the Bowling
Green to protest the
Stamp Act, New York City,
1765.

six black rebellions, from South Carolina to New York, and forty other riots.

But by the 1760s the colonies also had people we call local elites. These were political and social leaders in their city, town, or colony. Most of them were educated people, such as lawyers, doctors, and writers. Their thoughts carried weight. Some of these elite colonists were close to the ruling circles, made up of governors, tax collectors, and other officials who represented Great Britain. Other elite colonists were outside the ruling circles, but their fellow colonists looked up to them anyway.

These local elites were disturbed by the rising disorder. They feared that if the social order of the colonies were overturned, their own property and importance could be harmed. Then the elites saw a way to protect themselves and their positions. They could turn the rebellious energy of the colonists against Britain and its officials. This discovery was not a plan or a simple decision. Instead, it took shape over a few years as the elites faced one crisis after another.

## Anger and Violence

IN 1763 THE BRITISH DEFEATED FRANCE
in the Seven Years' War (called the French and
Indian War in the colonies). France no longer
threatened Britain's colonies in North America.
But after the war, the British government tight-
ened its control over those colonies, because they
were valuable. Britain needed taxes from the
colonists to help pay for the war. Also, trade with
the colonies brought large profits to Great Britain
every year.

But unemployment and poverty were rising in
the colonies. Poor people wandered the streets,
begging. At the same time, the richest colonists
controlled fortunes worth millions in today's dollars. There were many very poor people but only a
few very rich people.

Hardship made some colonists restless, even
rebellious. In the countryside, where most people
lived, poor and rich came into conflict. From the
1740s to the 1760s, tenants rioted and rebelled
against landlords in New York and New Jersey.

White farmers in North Carolina formed a
"Regulator Movement" in 1766. The Regulators
called themselves poor peasants and laborers. They

♦

claimed to stand for the common people against rich, powerful officials who governed unfairly. The Regulators were angry about high taxes. They also resented lawyers and merchants taking poor people to court over debts. When Regulators organized to keep taxes from being collected, the governor used military force against them. In May 1771, an army with cannon defeated several thousand Regulators. Six Regulators were hanged.

In Boston, the lower classes started using town meetings to air their complaints. One governor of Massachusetts wrote that Boston's poor people and common folk came regularly to the meetings. There were so many of them that they outvoted the "Gentlemen" and other Bostonians close to the ruling circle.

Something important was happening in Boston. It started with men like James Otis and Samuel Adams. They belonged to the local elite, but they were not part of the ruling group that was tied to Britain. Otis, Adams, and other local leaders recognized the feelings of the poorer Bostonians. Through powerful speeches and written articles, they stirred up those angry feelings and called the lower classes into action.

The Boston mob showed what it could do after
the British government passed the Stamp Act of
1765. This law taxed the colonists to pay for the
Seven Years' War. Colonists had already suffered
during the war, and now they didn't want to pay
for it. Crowds destroyed the homes of a rich merchant and of Thomas Hutchinson, one of those
who ruled in the name of Britain. They smashed
Hutchinson's house with axes, drank his wine,
and carried off his furniture and other belongings.

Officials reported to Britain that the destruction of Hutchinson's property was part of a plan to
attack other rich people. It was to be "a War of
Plunder, of general levelling and taking away the
Distinction of rich and poor." But such outbursts
worried local leaders like James Otis. They wanted
the class hatred of the poor to be turned only
against the rich who served the British—not
against themselves.

A group of Boston merchants, shipowners, and
master craftsmen formed a political group called the
Loyal Nine. They set up a march to protest the Stamp
Act. The Loyal Nine belonged to the upper and middle classes, but they encouraged lower-class people
such as shipworkers, apprentices, and craftsmen to

join their protest (but they did not include blacks). Two or three thousand people demonstrated outside a local official's home. But after the "gentlemen" who planned and organized the protest left, the crowd went further and destroyed some of the official's property. Later, the leaders said that the violence was wrong. They turned against the crowd and cut all ties with the rioters.

The next time the British government tried to tax the colonies, the colonial elites called for more demonstrations. But this time leaders like Samuel Adams and James Otis insisted, "No Mobs—No Confusions—No Tumults." (A "tumult" was a riot.) They wanted the people to show their anger against Britain, but they also wanted "Persons and Properties" to remain safe.

### Revolution in the Air

AS TIME WENT ON, FEELING AGAINST the British grew stronger. After 1768, two thousand British troops were stationed in Boston. At a time when jobs were scarce, these soldiers began taking the jobs of working people. On March 5, 1770, conflict between local workers and British soldiers broke into a tumult called the Boston Massacre.

Soldiers fired their guns at a crowd of demonstrators. They killed a mixed-race worker named Crispus Attucks, and then others. Colonist John Adams, a lawyer, defended the eight British soldiers at their trial. Adams called the crowd at the massacre "a motley rabble" and described it in scornful terms. Two of the soldiers were discharged from the army. The other six were found not guilty, which made some Bostonians even angrier. Britain took its troops out of the city, hoping things would quiet down.

But the colonists' anger did not go away. Political and social leaders in Boston formed a Committee of Correspondence to plan actions against the British. One of their actions was the Boston Tea Party of 1773. To protest the tax on tea, a group of colonists seized the cargo from a British ship and dumped it into Boston Harbor.

Britain's answer to the Boston Tea Party was a set of new, stricter laws. The British closed the port in Boston, broke up the colonial government, and sent in troops. Colonists held mass meetings of protest.

What about the other colonies? In Virginia, the educated elite wanted to turn the anger of the lower orders against Britain. They found a way in the speechmaking talents of Patrick Henry. In inspiring words, Henry told the colonists why they should be angry at Britain. At the same time, he avoided stirring up class conflict among the colonists. His words fed a feeling of patriotism, a growing resistance against Britain.

Other inspiring words helped turn the resistance movement toward independence. In 1776 Thomas Paine published a pamphlet, or short book, called *Common Sense*. It boldly made the first claim that the colonies should be free of British control.

Paine argued that sticking to Great Britain would do the colonists no good and that separating from Britain would do them no harm. He reminded his readers of all the wars that Britain had dragged them into—and of the lives and money those wars had cost them. Finally he made a thundering statement:

Everything that is right or reasonable pleads for separation. The blood of the slain, the weeping voice of nature
cries, 'TIS TIME TO PART.'

*Common Sense* was the most popular pamphlet in colonial America. But it caused some
alarm in elite colonists like John Adams. These
elites supported the patriot cause of independence from Britain, but they didn't want to go too
far toward democracy. Rule by the people had to
be kept within limits, Adams thought, because
the masses made hasty, foolish decisions.

Thomas Paine did not belong to the elite class.
He came to America as a poor emigrant from
England. But once the Revolution started, he sepa-
rated himself from the crowd actions of the lower
classes. Still, Paine's words in *Common Sense*
became part of the myth of the Revolution—that it
was the movement of a united people.

# COMMON SENSE:

## ADDRESSED TO THE

# INHABITANTS

### OF

# AMERICA.

## On the following interesting

# SUBJECTS.

I. Of the Origin and Design of Government in general, with concise Remarks on the English Constitution.

II. Of Monarchy and Hereditary Succession.

III. Thoughts on the present State of American Affairs.

IV. Of the present Ability of America, with some miscellaneous Reflections.

Written by an ENGLISHMAN.

*By Thomas Paine*

---

Man knows no Master save creating HEAVEN,
Or those whom choice and common good ordain.
THOMSON.

---

PHILADELPHIA, Printed
And Sold by R. BELL, in Third-Street, 1776.

## Whose Independence?

EVERY HARSH ACT OF BRITISH CONTROL made the colonists more rebellious. By 1774 they had set up the Continental Congress. It was an illegal political body, but it was also a step toward independent government.

The first military clash between colonists and British troops came at Lexington and Concord in April 1775. Afterward, the Continental Congress decided on separation from Great Britain. Thomas Jefferson wrote a Declaration of Independence. The Congress adopted it on July 2, 1776, and announced it two days later.

Throughout the colonies, there was already a strong feeling for independence. The opening words of the Declaration gave shape to that feeling:

> We hold these truths to be self-evident, that all men are created equal, that they are endowed by their Creator with certain unalienable Rights, that among these are Life, Liberty and the pursuit of Happiness—That to secure these rights, Governments are instituted among Men, deriving their just powers from the consent of the governed—That whenever any Form of Government becomes destructive of these ends, it is the Right of the People to alter or to abolish it, and to institute new Government....

*(left)*
Title page of Thomas Paine's revolutionary pamphlet "Common Sense," 1776.

Next, the Declaration listed the unjust or harmful acts of the British king. It described his rule as tyranny, or oppression—that is, rule by force, without fairness. The Declaration called for the people to control their government. It reminded them of the burdens and difficulties Britain had caused them. This language was well suited to bring various groups of colonists together. It could even make those who were at odds with each other turn against Britain.

But the Declaration did not include Indians, enslaved blacks, or women. As for the Indians, just twenty years earlier the government of Massachusetts had called them "rebels, enemies and traitors" and offered cash for each Indian scalp.

Black slaves were a problem for the author of the Declaration. At first, Jefferson's Declaration blamed the king for sending slaves to America, and also for not letting the colonies limit the slave trade. Maybe this statement grew out of moral feelings against slavery. Maybe it came from the fear of slave revolts. But the Continental Congress removed it from the Declaration of Independence because slaveholders in the colonies disagreed among themselves about whether or not to end slavery. So

Jefferson's gesture toward the enslaved black was left out of the Revolution's statement of freedom.

"All men are created equal," claimed the Declaration. Jefferson probably didn't use the word "men" on purpose, to leave out women. He just didn't think of including them. Women were invisible in politics. They had no political rights and no claim to equality.

By its own language, the Declaration of Independence limited life, liberty, and happiness to white males. But the makers and signers of the Declaration were like other people of their time. Their ideas grew out of the ordinary thinking of their age. We don't study the Declaration of Independence so that we can point out its moral failures. We study it so we can see how the Declaration drew certain groups of Americans into action while it ignored others. In our time, inspiring words are still used to get large numbers of people to support a cause, even while the same language covers up serious conflicts among people or leaves out whole parts of the human race.

The reality behind the Declaration of Independence was that a rising class of important people in the colonies needed enough support to defeat England. At the same time, they didn't want to disturb too much of the settled order of wealth and power. In fact, the makers of independence were part of that settled order. More than two-thirds of the men who signed the Declaration had served as colonial officials under the British.

When the fiery Declaration of Independence was read from Boston's town hall, the reader was Thomas Crafts. He was one of the Loyal Nine, who had opposed militant action against the British. Four days later, Boston's Committee of Correspondence ordered the town's men to show up to be drafted into a new patriot army. But the rich, it turned out, could avoid the draft. They could pay someone else to serve in the army for them. The poor had no choice but to serve. This led to rioting and shouting: "Tyranny is tyranny, let it come from whom it may."

# CHAPTER FIVE

# REVOLUTIONS

THE REVOLUTIONARY WAR WAS FOUGHT
between Great Britain and its colonies in North
America. But other rebellions took place during the
revolutionary years. Soldiers turned against their
officers, Indians sided with their old enemies, and
poor farmers in Massachusetts took up arms
against their brand-new American government.

## War and Mutiny

JOHN ADAMS, THE MASSACHUSETTS
lawyer who defended the soldiers who had fired in
the Boston Massacre, believed that only a third of

the people in the colonies supported the Revolution. A modern historian named John Shy, who studied the Revolutionary Army, thinks that only about a fifth of the total population actively turned against Britain.

But just about every white male in the colonies had a gun and could shoot. The leaders of the Revolution distrusted mobs of the poor, but they needed their help if they were going to beat Britain. How could the Revolutionary leaders win more people to their cause? One way to win support was by offering the rewards of military service. Men from the lower classes joined the army hoping to rise in rank, gain some money, and move up in society.

Historian Shy found that poor people "did much of the actual fighting and suffering" in the Revolution. Not all of them were volunteers. Just a few years earlier, colonists had rioted against the British practice of impressment, seizing men and forcing them to serve in the navy. But by 1779, in the middle of the Revolution, the American navy was doing the same thing.

The Americans lost the first battles of the war, at Bunker Hill and Brooklyn Heights. They won

*(left)*
Blacksmith being served a tax writ, 1786.

small battles at Trenton and Princeton, then a big battle at Saratoga, New York, in 1777. While George Washington's frozen army hung on at Valley Forge, Pennsylvania, Benjamin Franklin was in France, looking for help. Britain had defeated France in the Seven Years' War, and the French were hungry for revenge. They joined the war on the American side.

The war moved to the South. The British won victory after victory, until British and American armies met at Yorktown, Virginia, in 1781. With the help of a large French army, and with the French navy blocking the British from getting more men or supplies, the Americans won this final victory, and the war was over.

Throughout the war, rich and poor Americans came into conflict. Rich men led the Continental Congress, which governed the colonies. These men were connected to each other by marriage and family relationships, and also by business ties. They looked out for each other.

The Congress voted that army officers who stuck to the end of the war would receive half their military pay for the rest of their lives. This ignored the common soldiers, who were not getting paid.

On New Year's Day, 1781, some Pennsylvania troops mutinied. They killed one of their captains, wounded others, and marched with cannon toward Philadelphia and the Congress. George Washington, commander of the army, made peace with the rebellious soldiers.

Soon afterward, when soldiers mutinied in New Jersey, Washington took a sterner stand. He ordered two of the ringleaders shot by firing squads made up of their friends, who cried as they pulled the triggers. It was "an example," Washington said.

Soldiers' mutinies were rare. Rebellion was easier for people who were not in the army. Civil disorder flared up in half a dozen colonies, even while the colonies were fighting against Great Britain.

In the southern colonies, the lower classes did not want to join the Revolution. They thought the war had nothing to do with them. Whether or not the colonies won independence from Britain, they would still be ruled by a political elite.

Nathanael Greene, Washington's general in the South, wrote a letter to Thomas Jefferson telling how his troops dealt with some Loyalists, colonists who had remained loyal to Britain. Greene wrote that "upwards of one hundred were killed and most of the rest cut to pieces." He added that this action had a "happy effect" on people in the area who had held back from supporting the Revolution.

Tenant farmers became a threatening force during the war. These farmers paid rent to landlords who owned huge estates. When they stopped paying rent, the Revolutionary government feared a rebellion. So the government seized Loyalists' land and sold some of it to tenants. These new landholders no longer had to pay rent—but now they had to pay the banks that had loaned them money to buy land.

Much property taken from Loyalists went to enrich the Revolutionary leaders and their friends. The Revolution gave these colonial elites a chance to seize power and property from those who had been loyal to Britain. The war also gave some benefits to small landholders. But for most poor white working people and tenant farmers, the Revolution brought little change.

## Indians and Blacks in the Revolution

IN THE SEVEN YEARS' WAR BETWEEN
Britain and France, many of the Indians of
North America had fought on the side of
France. The French were traders who did not
try to take over Indian lands, but the British
wanted living space.

After the Seven Years' War, the French ignored
their Indian allies and gave French territory in the
Ohio Valley to the British. There the Indians
attacked British forts, and the British fought back.
One of their weapons was biological warfare.
They gave the Indians blankets from a hospital,
hoping to spread the deadly disease smallpox
among the tribes.

But the British could not destroy the will of the
Indians, so in 1763 they made peace. Britain
declared that the land west of the Appalachian
Mountains was Indian territory. Colonists were
forbidden to settle there. This angered the
colonists and gave them another reason to turn
against Britain. It also explains why many Indians
fought on the side of the British, their old enemies, during the Revolution. After the war, with
the British out of the way, the Americans could

begin pushing the Indians off their lands, killing them if they fought back.

Black slaves also fought in the Revolution—on both sides. Blacks seeking freedom offered to fight in the Revolutionary Army. George Washington turned them down. In the end, though, about five thousand blacks served with the Revolutionaries. Thousands more fought for the British.

The Revolution encouraged some blacks to demand more from white society. In 1780, for example, seven blacks in Massachusetts asked the legislature for the right to vote. They pointed out that Americans had just been fighting a war for the right to govern themselves, and they reminded lawmakers that many "of our Colour" had fought for the Revolutionary cause.

After the war, slavery ended in the northern states—but slowly. In 1810 about thirty thousand people remained enslaved in the North. By 1840 there were still a thousand slaves. In the lower South, slavery expanded with the growth of rice and cotton plantations.

*(left)*
Revolutionary War
soldiers, 1780.

## Farmers in Revolt

BY THE TIME OF THE REVOLUTION,
certain patterns were already set in the American
colonies. Indians had no place in the new society.
Blacks were not treated as the equals of whites.
The rich and powerful ran things. After the war,
the Revolutionary leaders could make those patterns into the law of the new nation.

A group of leaders met in Philadelphia in 1787
to write the United States Constitution. Hanging
over them was the fear of revolt. The year before, a
farmers' uprising called Shays' Rebellion had
turned western Massachusetts into a battleground.

Massachusetts had passed state laws that
raised the property qualifications for voting.
People couldn't vote if they didn't own enough
land. In addition, only the very wealthy could hold
state office. Farmers who could not pay their debts
were angry that the state lawmakers did nothing to
help them.

A countryman named Plough Jogger spoke up
at a meeting to say how the government had mistreated him—and what he wanted to do about it:

> I have been greatly abused, have been obliged to do more
> than my part in the war; have been loaded with class rates

[taxes], town rates, province rates, Continental rates and all rates . . . been pulled and hauled by sheriffs, constables and [tax] collectors, and had my cattle sold for less than they were worth. . . . The great men are going to get all we have and I think it is time for us to rise up and put a stop to it, and have no more courts, nor sheriffs, nor collectors nor lawyers. . . .

Some of the discontented farmers were veterans of the Continental Army. They had fought for the Revolutionary cause, but when the war ended, they did not receive their pay in cash. They were in debt, but they had no money. When the courts met to take away their cattle and land, the farmers protested. Large, armed groups marched to courthouse steps, keeping the courts from carrying out their actions. Farmers' mobs also broke into jails to free imprisoned debtors.

The political leaders of Massachusetts became alarmed. Samuel Adams, who had acted against the British government in Boston, now insisted that people stay within the law. People in the town of Greenwich answered back. They said: You in Boston have the money. We don't. And didn't you act illegally yourselves in the Revolution?

Daniel Shays was a poor farm hand when the

Revolution broke out. He joined the army and fought at Lexington, Bunker Hill, and Saratoga. In 1780 he quit the army because he had not been paid. Back home, he found himself in court because he couldn't pay his debts. He saw the same thing happening to others. One sick woman, unable to pay, had her bed taken from under her.

When the Massachusetts Supreme Court charged leaders of the farmers' rebellion with crimes, Shays organized seven hundred armed farmers, mostly veterans. As they marched toward Springfield and the court, others joined them. The judges cut the court session short.

The farmers kept up the pressure, but winter snows began to interfere with their trips to the courthouses. When Shays marched a thousand men toward Boston, a storm forced them back, and one man froze to death. Then Boston merchants raised money to pay for an army to take the field against the farmers. The rebels were outnumbered and on the run. Shays fled to Vermont. Some of his followers surrendered. A few died in battle. Others carried out desperate acts of violence against authority, such as burning barns or killing a general's horse.

Captured rebels were put on trial. Although Shays was later pardoned, a dozen were sentenced to die. Sam Adams claimed that there was a difference between rebelling against a king, as he had done, and the farmers' uprising. Treason against a king might be pardoned, Adams said, "but the man who dares rebel against the laws of a republic ought to suffer death."

Thomas Jefferson felt differently. He thought that such uprisings were healthy for society. Jefferson wrote, "I hold it that a little rebellion now and then is a good thing. . . . It is a medicine necessary for the sound health of government."

But the political and economic leaders of the new nation did not share Jefferson's view. They feared that revolt would spread, and that the poor would demand a share of the rich people's property. These fears were in the minds of those who wrote the U.S. Constitution.

## The Constitution—Business as Usual

MANY AMERICANS HAVE SEEN THE
Constitution as a work of genius, put together by
wise men who created a legal framework for
democracy and equality. But there is another way
to look at it.

In 1935, historian Charles Beard put forward a
view of the Constitution that angered some people.
Beard studied the fifty-five men who met to write
the Constitution. He found that most were wealthy.
Half of them were moneylenders, and many were
lawyers. They had reasons to create a strong federal,
or central, government that could protect the economic system that they understood and were part
of. Beard also noted that no women, blacks, indentured servants, or people without property helped
write the Constitution. So the Constitution did not
reflect the interests of those groups.

The Constitution said that each state's lawmakers would elect the senators who would represent
that state in the federal Congress. The state lawmakers would also choose electors, who would
elect the president. The president would name the
members of the Supreme Court. The only part of
the government that the people would elect

directly was the U.S. House of Representatives.
Even in those elections, each state set its own voting requirements. Women, Indians, and slaves
could not vote. In almost every state, men without
property could not vote, either.

The problem of democracy went deeper than
the Constitution's limits on voting. It lay in the
division of society into rich and poor. Some people
had great wealth and power. They owned and controlled the land, the money, the newspapers, the
churches, and the educational system. How could
voting cut into such power?

The time came for the states to ratify the
Constitution—to accept it and make it the new
national law. Some people wanted the
Constitution and its strong central government.
Others felt that the thirteen states should remain
independent or loosely connected.

In New York, debate over ratification was
intense. Supporters of the Constitution were
called Federalists. One of the leading Federalists
was Alexander Hamilton, who believed that society was naturally divided into classes. In
Hamilton's view, the upper class should run
things, because true democracy was dangerous:

All communities divide themselves into the few and the
many. The first are the rich and well-born, the other the
mass of the people. . . . The people are turbulent and
changing; they seldom judge or determine right. Give
therefore to the first class a distinct permanent share in
the government. . . . Nothing but a permanent body can
check the imprudence of democracy. . . .

The Federalists published papers explaining
the advantages of a central government. One
advantage, said James Madison, was that riots,
revolts, and civil disorder would be less likely to
arise in "a large nation ranging over thirteen
states" than in a single state. People's desire for
such "wicked" things as "an equal division of
property" might overcome a state government, but
not a federal one.

About a third of the people in the United
States owned some property. Most of them
owned only small amounts of land. Still, one-
third of the population felt they had something
that a strong, stable government could protect.
In addition, crafts workers in the cities wanted
a central government that could protect their
jobs by taxing imported goods. This was a
larger base of support for government than

anywhere else in the world at the end of the eighteenth century.

The Constitution served the interests of a wealthy elite. But it also did enough for small property owners and middle-income workers and farmers to win their support. The Constitution became even more acceptable after Congress passed the amendments, or changes, known as the Bill of Rights. The Bill of Rights seemed to make the new government a protector of people's liberties. It guaranteed the right to speak, to publish, to worship, to be tried fairly, and so on. It also guaranteed the right of habeas corpus, which means that no one can be imprisoned without a hearing. But the First Amendment shows how quickly liberty could be taken away.

The First Amendment says that Congress will make no law that limits freedom of speech or of the press. But in 1798, just seven years after the Bill of Rights was added to the Constitution, Congress passed a law that clearly limited the right of free speech.

That law was the Sedition Act, which made it a crime to say anything "false, scandalous and malicious" against the federal government. Criticism that might turn the people against the government was forbidden. The Sedition Act seemed to violate the First Amendment, but ten people went to prison for saying things against the government.

Congress also passed new taxes to pay for war bonds. Although society's richest people owned most of the bonds, ordinary people had to pay the taxes. One law, the Whiskey Tax, hurt small farmers who made whiskey to sell. When farmers took up arms against the tax in 1794, the government sent troops to put down the rebellion. Even in the early years of the Constitution, some parts of it, such as the First Amendment, could be treated lightly. Other parts, such as the power to tax, were powerfully enforced.

Were the Founding Fathers wise and just men trying to create a balance of power? They did not want a balance, except one that kept things as they were. They certainly did not want an equal balance between slave and master, rich and poor, or Indian and white. Half the people in the country were not even considered by the Founding Fathers. These "invisible" citizens were the women of early America.

# CHAPTER SIX

# THE WOMEN
# OF EARLY AMERICA

SOME HISTORY BOOKS MAKE IT LOOK
as if half the people in America never even
existed. History books talk about explorers, merchants, politicians, and generals—but these are all
men. In early America, women couldn't hold any
of those jobs. They were invisible to history.

For the European people who settled the
Americas, law and social customs said clearly that
women were not the equals of men. Fathers and
husbands had the right to control women. Women
were oppressed, which means that they could not
control their own lives. The oppression of women
would be hard to uproot.

## How Women Were Treated

THE FIRST SETTLEMENTS IN THE AMERICAN colonies were made up almost completely of men. Women were brought in to be wives, childbearers, and companions. In 1619, a ship arrived at the colony of Jamestown, Virginia, carrying ninety women. They had agreed to come to the colony to marry men they had never met, in exchange for the cost of their passage across the Atlantic Ocean.

Many women and teenaged girls came to the colonies as indentured servants. Their lives were not very different from slaves' lives, except that their service had an end. While they were servants, they had to obey their masters and mistresses, and they sometimes experienced sexual abuse. Female servants "were poorly paid and often treated rudely and harshly," according to a history called *America's Working Women.*

Black women suffered doubly. They were oppressed as blacks *and* as women. A slave trader reported on the terrible conditions they endured crossing the Atlantic:

> I saw pregnant women giving birth to babies while chained to corpses which our drunken overseers had not removed. . . . On board the ship was a young negro

woman chained to the deck, who had lost her senses soon after she was purchased and taken on board.

Even free white women faced hardships. Giving birth and raising children were difficult in a time when medical care was poor and disease was common. Eighteen married women came to America on the *Mayflower*, the Pilgrims' ship. Three were pregnant. Less than a year later, only four of the women were alive. Childbirth and sickness had taken the others.

Laws and ideas carried over from England were another burden for women. Under the law, when a woman married, her husband became her master. Husbands had the legal right to control their wives in every way. A man could physically punish his wife (although he could not kill her or give her a permanent injury). Her property and possessions became his. If she earned money, that was his, too.

*Advice to a Daughter* was a bestselling English book. It claimed that "Inequality in Sexes" was a fact of life. Many Americans read this book, which said that men were meant to be the lawgivers and that they had more power of reason—more thinking ability—than did women. But in spite of powerful

messages that women were inferior to men, some women found ways to show their independence.

## Independent Women

ANNE HUTCHINSON WAS A RELIGIOUS woman in the early years of the Massachusetts Bay Colony. She stood up to the church fathers by insisting that she could read the Bible and figure out its meaning for herself, and so could other ordinary people.

Hutchinson went to trial twice. The church put her on trial for heresy, the crime of holding beliefs that were not approved by the religious leaders. The government of the colony put her on trial for standing up against its authority.

Hutchinson was ordered to leave the Massachusetts Bay Colony. When she left for Rhode Island in 1638, thirty-five other families followed her. Later Hutchinson went to Long Island. Indians there thought that she was one of the enemies who had cheated them out of their land, and they killed

*(left)*
"Anne Hutchinson Preaches," 20th Century.

her and her family. Another woman in the Massachusetts Bay Colony, Mary Dyer, was hanged because of her "rebellious" beliefs and behavior.

Few women took part in public affairs such as politics. But during the American Revolution, the pressures of war brought some women into public life. Women formed patriotic groups, carried out anti-British actions, and wrote articles for independence.

In 1777, women even had their own version of the Boston Tea Party. Abigail Adams described it in a letter to her husband John Adams, a lawyer and one of the Founding Fathers. When a rich merchant refused to sell coffee at a fair price, a band of women marched to his warehouse. After one of the women threw the merchant into a cart, he handed over his keys, and the women helped themselves to the coffee and left. Abigail Adams wrote, "A large concourse of men stood amazed, silent spectators of the whole transaction."

On the frontier, when skill and labor were in short supply, some women had the chance to prove that they were equal to men. Before and after the Revolution, they worked at important jobs, such as publishing newspapers, running shops, and managing inns. Other women—and children, too—worked in their homes, spinning thread for local plants to weave into cloth.

When industry started to be an important part of the economy, women were pulled out of the home and into factory jobs. But at the same time, there was pressure for women to stay at home where they could be more easily controlled.

What some claimed to be the perfect woman began to appear in sermons and books. Her job was to keep the home cheerful, religious, and patriotic. She was supposed to be her family's nurse, cook, cleaner, seamstress, teacher, and flower arranger. She shouldn't read too much— and certain books must be avoided. Above all, a woman's role was to meet her husband's needs.

## Women at Work

WHILE PREACHERS AND WRITERS WERE PRAISING proper "womanly" behavior, women started pushing against the limits that society set on what they

Striking Women, 1860.

could do. They couldn't vote or own property. They couldn't go to college or study law and medicine. If they worked, their wages would be much less than men's, for the same jobs.

But women *were* going to work. In the nineteenth century many of them found jobs in textile, or clothmaking factories, where they operated new industrial machines such as power looms. Out of every ten textile workers, eight or nine were women. Most of those women were between fifteen and thirty years old.

These working women led some of the first industrial strikes. They walked off their jobs in the textile mills to demand higher wages and better working conditions. The earliest known strike of female factory workers came in 1824, in Pawtucket, Rhode Island. Ten years later, when a young woman was fired from her job in Lowell, Massachusetts, other young women left their looms in protest. One of them climbed onto the town pump and made a fiery speech about the rights of women.

Catherine Beecher was in Lowell at that time. Beecher later became a reformer who worked to improve education for women. She wrote about the mill system that inspired the women's revolt:

> I was there in mid-winter, and every morning I was awak-
> ened at five, by the bells calling to labor. . . . Then half an
> hour only allowed for dinner, from which the time for
> going and returning was deducted. Then back to the mills,
> to work till seven o'clock. . . . [I]t must be remembered that
> all the hours of labor are spent in rooms where oil lamps,
> together with from 40 to 80 persons, are exhausting the
> healthful principle of the air . . . and where the air is
> loaded with particles of cotton thrown from thousands of
> cards, spindles, and looms.

## Rights for Women?

THE TEXTILE MILLS WEREN'T THE ONLY
places where people were talking about women's
rights. The place of women in society was beginning, slowly, to change.

Middle-class women couldn't go to college, but
they could become teachers in primary schools.
They began to take over that profession. As teachers, they read more and communicated more.

Girls and women started to knock more loudly on the doors of higher education.

In 1821, Emma Willard founded the first school specially for girls. Twenty-eight years later, Elizabeth Blackwell became a pioneer when she managed to earn a medical degree.

Women also began to write for magazines, and they even started some women's magazines. Between 1780 and 1840, the percentage of American women who could read and write doubled. Women joined religious organizations and became health reformers. Some of the most powerful of them joined the antislavery movement.

Through all of these activities, women gained experience in organizing, giving speeches, and taking action for causes. Soon they would use that experience in a new cause: women's rights.

Lucy Stone was a lecturer for the American Anti-Slavery Society. She was a firm speaker who wasn't afraid to voice ideas that were unpopular. During her speeches Stone was soaked with cold water, struck by a thrown book, and attacked by mobs. Still, she started lecturing about women's rights in 1847, in a church in Massachusetts where her brother was a minister.

Angelina Grimké was another antislavery activist who turned to the cause of women's rights. She believed that if the United States could "lift up millions of slaves of both sexes from the dust, and turn them into men and women," then it could also take "millions of females from their knees and set them on their feet."

All over the country, women did an enormous amount of work for the antislavery societies. This helped inspire a movement for women's equality that raced alongside the movement against slavery. An important starting point for the women's rights movement was a World's Anti-Slavery Convention in London, England, in 1840.

The organizers of the meeting almost kept women from attending it at all, because it wasn't "proper" for women to go to public conventions. In the end, women were allowed to attend—but only if they sat behind a curtain. American abolitionist William Lloyd Garrison, who supported the rights of women as well as the end of slavery, sat with them.

Being treated as second-class members of the antislavery movement angered women such as Elizabeth Cady Stanton and Lucretia Mott. They were antislavery activists who became deeply concerned with the roles and rights of women in society.

Stanton and Mott organized the first women's rights convention in history. It took place in Stanton's hometown of Seneca Falls, New York, in 1848. Three hundred women came to the meeting. So did some men who were in favor of women's rights.

At the end of the convention, a hundred people signed a Declaration of Principles that used some of the language of Thomas Jefferson's Declaration of Independence—but changed to include women. The Declaration of Principles said that "all men and women are created equal." It described the unfair treatment of women and outlined steps toward greater equality.

But true equality would mean more than giving rights to women. It would mean treating black women equally with white women. In 1851, at a meeting in support of women's rights, an elderly black woman sat listening to some male ministers. They were doing most of the talking. Then she rose to her feet. Tall and thin, wearing a gray dress and a white turban, this former slave named Sojourner Truth told about her life as a black woman:

That man over there says that woman needs to be helped into carriages and lifted over ditches. . . . Nobody ever helps me into carriages, or over mud-puddles or gives me any best place. And a'nt I a woman?

Look at my arm! I have ploughed, and planted, and gathered into barns, and no man could head me! And a'nt I a woman?

I would work as much and eat as much as a man, when I could get it, and bear the lash as well. And a'nt I a woman?

I have born thirteen children and seen em most all sold off to slavery, and when I cried out with my mother's grief, none but Jesus heard me! And a'nt I a woman?

As other women held conventions around the country, the movement gained strength. Women were fighting back against those who wanted to keep them in "a woman's place." They took part in all sorts of movements—not just for women's rights but for prison reform, health care, and the end of slavery.

In the middle of all these movements, a new urge seized the United States. It was the urge to expand, to become larger. Americans wanted more land. They would take it from the Indians, as they had done from the start.

IN THE REVOLUTIONARY WAR, ALMOST
every important Indian nation fought on the side
of the British. They knew that if the British lost
the war, there would be no holding back the
Americans. Settlers would pour across the
Appalachian Mountains into Indian territory.

The Indians were right. By the time Thomas
Jefferson became president in 1800, about
700,000 white settlers were already living west of
the mountains. Americans were eager to fill up
the land between the Appalachians and the
Mississippi River. They wanted to cut forests,
plant cotton and grain, and build roads, cities, and
canals. In time, they came to think that their
nation should reach all the way across North
America to the Pacific Ocean.

The Indians stood in the way of these plans. So
the United States government came up with the
idea of "Indian removal" to clear the land so that
whites could use it. This "removal" cost a great
deal in lives and suffering. It is hard for historians
to measure this huge loss.

# CHAPTER SEVEN

# AS LONG AS GRASS GROWS OR WATER RUNS

## From Indian Fighter to President

AFTER THE REVOLUTION, RICH AMERICANS bought up huge pieces of land on the frontier. They planned to sell it later for great profits. This was called speculating. Some of the speculators were Founding Fathers, including George Washington and Patrick Henry.

Another land speculator was also a merchant, slave trader, soldier, and future president. He was Andrew Jackson, the harshest enemy of the Indians in early American history.

Jackson became famous during the War of 1812. Textbooks usually say that the war was a struggle against Britain for America's survival, but it was more than that. It was also a war for territory. It allowed the United States to expand into

Canada, into Florida (which was owned by Spain), and into Indian territory.

Jackson's first Indian wars were against the Creeks, who lived in most of Georgia, Alabama, and Mississippi. In the midst of the war, Creek warriors massacred 250 whites at an Alabama fort. Jackson's troops took revenge by burning down a Creek village, killing women and children as well as men. A year later, in 1814, Jackson became a national hero when he fought the Battle of Horseshoe Bend against a thousand Creeks. He killed eight hundred of them, with few deaths on his side. Jackson owed his victory to Cherokees who fought on his side because the government had promised to treat them well if they joined the war. Jackson's white troops failed in an attack on the Creeks, but the Cherokees swam a river, came up behind the Creeks, and won the battle for Jackson.

When the war ended, Jackson and his friends started buying up Creek lands. Jackson got himself put in charge of treaties. In 1814 he wrote a treaty that took away half the land of the Creek nation.

This treaty started something new and important. The Indians had never thought that land belonged to individual owners. As a Shawnee chieftain named Tecumseh said, "The land belongs to all, for the use of each. . . ." But Jackson's treaty gave the Indians individual owner-ship of land and broke up their shared landhold-ings. The treaty turned Indian against Indian, bribing some of them with land and leaving oth-ers out.

Over the next ten years, Jackson was involved in many more treaties with the southern Indians. Through force, bribery, and tricks, he helped whites takes over three-fourths of Alabama and Florida, a third of Tennessee, and parts of four other states. These land grabs became the basis for the cotton kingdom of the South, where slaves labored on white-owned plantations.

Soon white settlement reached the edge of Spanish Florida, home of the Seminole Indians and some escaped black slaves. Jackson claimed that the United States had to control Florida in order to defend itself—just what modern nations often say before starting a war of conquest in some other country's territory.

Jackson started making raids into Florida, burning Seminole villages and seizing Spanish forts. As a result of these attacks, Spain agreed to

sell Florida to the United States. Jackson became governor of the new territory. He also gave his friends and relatives advice on buying slaves and speculating in land.

In 1828, Americans elected Jackson president. Under Jackson and Martin Van Buren, the man he chose to follow him as president, the U.S. government removed seventy thousand Indians from their homelands east of the Mississippi River. A government official named Lewis Cass explained the removal by saying that "savages" could not live "in contact with a civilized community."

Cass had taken millions of acres from the Indians when he was governor of the Michigan Territory. In 1825, at a treaty meeting with the Shawnees and Cherokees, he had promised them that if they moved west, across the Mississippi River, "The United States will never ask for your land there." The land beyond the river, Cass declared, would remain Indian territory forever.

AS LONG AS GRASS GROWS OR WATER RUNS

*(left)*
Jackson & Weatherford,
19th century.

The Trail of Tears, 1838.

## The Terrible Choice

FOR A FEW YEARS IN THE 1820S, BEFORE Jackson became president, the southern Indians and whites had settled down. They lived in peace, often close to one another. White men visited Indian communities, and Indians were guests in white homes. Frontier figures like Davy Crockett and Sam Houston came out of this setting. Both of them—unlike Andrew Jackson—were friends of the Indians.

Pressure to remove the Indians from the land came from politicians, business interests, land speculators, and population growth that demanded new railroads and cities. These pressures might push poor white frontiersmen into the first violent clashes with the Indians, but the frontiersmen who were neighbors of the Indians did not lead the movement to get rid of them.

Just *how* did the government remove the Indians from Georgia, Alabama, Mississippi, and other places? The answer lies in the difference between federal (or national) laws and state laws. Federal laws, like treaties between the federal government and the tribes, put the U.S. Congress in charge of Indian affairs. But the states passed their own laws that gave away Indian land to whites.

As president, Jackson was supposed to enforce the federal laws. Instead he ignored them, letting the states do what they wanted. This put the Indians in a terrible position. They would not be "forced" to go west. But if they stayed, they would have to obey state laws, which destroyed their rights. They would suffer endless trouble from whites who wanted their land.

On the other hand, if the Indians agreed to leave, the federal government would help them with money and give them land west of the Mississippi. Jackson told the Choctaws and Cherokees that if they left their old lands peacefully, they would be given new lands, and the government would leave them alone. He sent them this message:

> Say to the chiefs and warriors that I am their friend . . . but they must, by removing from the limits of the States of Mississippi and Alabama and by being settled on the lands I offer them, put it in my power to be such—There, beyond the limits of any State, in possession of land of their own, which they shall possess as long as Grass grows or water runs. I am and will protect them and be their friend and father.

Now the pressures began on the tribes, one by one. The Choctaws didn't want to leave, but after fifty members of the tribe were bribed with money and land, they signed a treaty that gave up Choctaw lands east of the Mississippi. In return, the Choctaws were supposed to get financial help for the journey west. Thirteen thousand of them began that journey in late 1831, migrating to a land and climate completely different from everything they knew. The army was supposed to organize their trip, but it failed miserably. Indians died by the thousands from hunger, cold, and disease. The seven thousand Choctaws still in Mississippi refused to follow them. Some of their descendants still live in Mississippi.

After Jackson was re-elected to the presidency in 1832, he speeded up what was called the Indian removal. By this time, Alabama's twenty-two thousand Creeks lived on a tiny portion of their former territory. They agreed to leave in exchange for the federal government's promise that some of that land would be given to individual Creeks, who could either sell it or stay on it with federal protection.

The government immediately broke its promise. It didn't protect Creeks from whites who swarmed onto their land. An army officer wrote that the Creeks were "brow beat, and cowed, and imposed upon, and depressed with the feeling that they have no adequate protection in the United States. . . ."

Speckled Snake was a man of the Creek nation. During his long life, he saw the white American government cheat and mistreat the Indians over and over again. When he was more than a hundred years old, he told a story about how the white man had betrayed the Indian:

> Brothers! I have listened to many talks from our great white father. When he first came over the wide waters, he was but a little man . . . very little. His legs were cramped by sitting long in his big boat, and he begged for a little land to light his fire on. . . . But when the white man had warmed himself before the Indians' fire and filled himself with their hominy, he became very large. With a step he bestrode the mountains, and his feet covered the plains and the valleys. His hand grasped the eastern and the western sea, and his head rested on the moon. Then he became our Great Father. He loved his red children, and he said, "Get a little further, lest I tread on thee."

After some desperate Creeks attacked white settlers, the government claimed that this "war" had broken the treaty. Now the U.S. Army could use force to make the Creeks go west. Soldiers invaded Creek communities and marched the people westward in groups of two or three thousand. The government was supposed to supply things like food, shelter, and blankets to the marchers, but again it failed. Starvation and sickness killed hundreds as the Creeks were carried across the Mississippi on old, rotting boats. More than three hundred Indians died when one boat sank.

## Fighting for Freedom

IN DECEMBER 1835 A GOVERNMENT OFFICIAL ordered the Seminoles of Florida to gather at a meeting place to begin their journey west. No one showed up. The Seminoles had decided to fight.

They started making surprise attacks on white settlements along the coast, striking quickly from hideouts in the interior. They murdered white families, captured slaves, and destroyed property. General Winfield Scott led U.S. troops into Florida to fight the Seminoles, but they found no one. Two-thirds of Scott's officers resigned from the army, worn out by mud, swamps, heat, and disease.

The war lasted eight years and cost $20 million and 1,500 American lives. But the Seminoles were a tiny force fighting a huge nation that had great resources. Finally, in the 1840s, they got tired. The Seminoles asked for a truce but were arrested. Their leader Osceola, died in prison, and the war died out.

In Georgia, the Cherokees were fighting back in their own way, without violence. They tried to fit into the white man's world by becoming farm-ers, blacksmiths, and carpenters. They set up a governing council and welcomed Christianity and white missionaries. After their chief, Sequoyah, invented a written form of their language, they printed a newspaper in both English and Cherokee. But although the Cherokees were tak-ing up the ways of white society, the whites still wanted their land.

Georgia passed laws that stripped the Cherokees of their land and outlawed the tribal government, meetings, and newspaper. Any Indian who encouraged others to stay in the homeland could go to prison. White missionaries who said that the Cherokees should be allowed to remain on their land also received punishments such as four years at hard labor in prison.

Once again, the federal government arranged a removal treaty with a few Cherokees, who signed it behind the backs of most of the tribe. And once again the government sent the army to enforce the treaty. Seventeen thousand Cherokees were rounded up and crowded into stockades. On October 1, 1838, the first group set out on what came to be called the Trail of Tears.

Four thousand Cherokees died of hunger, thirst, sickness, or exposure in the stockades or on the brutal march westward. But in December 1838, President Martin Van Buren told Congress about "the entire removal of the Cherokee Nation of Indians to their new homes west of the Mississippi." Congress's decision to remove the Cherokees, Van Buren said, had had "the happiest effects."

# CHAPTER EIGHT

# WAR WITH MEXICO

"I HAVE SCARCELY SLEPT A WINK,"
Ethan Allen Hitchcock wrote in his diary on June
30, 1845. Hitchcock was a colonel in the U.S.
Army, stationed in Louisiana. His commander,
General Zachary Taylor, had just been ordered to
lead his men to the banks of the Rio Grande, a
river on the southwest side of Texas. Hitchcock
knew that this would bring trouble.

"Violence leads to violence," he wrote, "and if
this movement of ours does not lead to others and
to bloodshed, I am much mistaken." Hitchcock
was not mistaken. Taylor's march to the Rio
Grande started a bloody war—a war that gave
Americans a huge new western territory, taken
from a defeated Mexico.

## Manifest Destiny

EVEN THOUGH THOMAS JEFFERSON'S Louisiana Purchase of 1803 had doubled the size of the United States, the country was a lot smaller in 1845 than it is today. Its western border was the Rocky Mountains. To the southwest was Mexico, which had won its independence from Spain in 1821.

Mexico was originally much larger than it is now. It included Texas, New Mexico, Utah, Nevada, Arizona, California, and parts of Colorado and Wyoming. Then, with help from the United States, Texas broke away from Mexico in 1836, calling itself the "Lone Star Republic." In 1845, the U.S. Congress added Texas to the United States.

By that time, many Americans believed that their country should expand, or grow larger, toward the west. One of these expansionists was President James Polk. He told his secretary that one of his main goals as president was to get California into the United States. A newspaper called the *Washington Union* supported Polk's idea with these words: "The road to California will be open to us. Who will stay [meaning halt, or stop] the march of our western people?"

Soon afterward, in the summer of 1845, another newspaper editor, John O'Sullivan, wrote, "Our manifest destiny [is] to overspread the continent allotted by Providence for the free development of our yearly multiplying millions." O'Sullivan was saying that Americans should be free to occupy all of North America, because God meant for them to. His words "manifest destiny"—a fate or purpose that was clear to see— became a slogan for expansionists.

For a long time, Mexico and the United States had agreed that the border between them was the Nueces River, about 150 miles north of the Rio Grande. But during Texas's fight for independence from Mexico, Texans had captured the Mexican general Santa Anna and forced him to say that the border was the Rio Grande. This made Texas bigger. Afterward, President Polk promised the Texans that he would consider the Rio Grande the border, even though Mexicans still lived in the area between the two rivers.

So when Polk ordered General Taylor to move troops to the Rio Grande, he was challenging Mexico. Sending the army into territory inhabited by Mexicans was sure to cause conflict. But when

the soldiers reached the Rio Grande, they found empty villages. The local Mexicans had fled across the river to the city of Matamoros. Taylor started building a fort with cannons pointed at Matamoros.

By the spring of 1846, the army was ready to start the war that Polk wanted. All it needed was an excuse. Then one of Taylor's officers disappeared while riding along the river. He was later found with a smashed skull. Everyone figured that Mexican guerrilla fighters had crossed the river and killed him. The very next day, Mexicans attacked a patrol, killing sixteen soldiers. Taylor sent a message to Polk that the fighting had begun.

The Mexicans had fired the first shot. But they had done what the American government wanted. Colonel Ethan Allan Hitchcock knew that. Even before the attacks, he wrote in his diary:

> I have said from the first that the United States are the aggressors. . . . We have not one particle of right to be here. . . . It looks as if the government sent a small force on purpose to bring on a war, so as to have a pretext [reason] for taking California and as much of this country as it chooses. . . . My heart is not in this business . . . but, as a military man, I am bound to execute orders.

*(left)*
Mexican War Cartoon, 1846.

## For and Against the War

PRESIDENT POLK HAD BEEN URGING
Congress to declare war even before he received
word of the attacks from General Taylor. As soon
as Taylor's messages arrived, Polk told Congress,
"Mexico has passed the boundary of the United
States, has invaded our territory and shed
American blood upon the American soil. . . ."

Congress declared war. Only a handful of con-
gressmen voted against it. They were strongly
opposed to slavery, and they believed that the war
was an excuse to gain territory that would be made
into new slave states. Joshua Giddings of Ohio
called it "an aggressive, unholy, and unjust war."

Many Americans cheered the news of war.
They held rallies to support it in cities across the
land, and they volunteered for the army by the
thousands. The poet Walt Whitman wrote proudly
in a newpaper that "America knows how to crush,
as well as how to expand!"

Another poet, James Russell Lowell, took a different view of the war. He wrote a poem saying
that the only reason for it was "to lug new slave
states in." Massachusetts writer Henry David
Thoreau criticized the war. He was also jailed for

refusing to pay a poll tax, but he only spent one night there. He was released because his friends paid the tax for him, without his permission.

Two years later, Thoreau wrote an essay called "Civil Disobedience." It talks about the difference between law and justice, and about how soldiers sometimes know that the orders they are following are wrong:

> Law never made men a whit more just; and, by means of their respect for it, even the well-disposed are daily made the agents of injustice. A common and natural result of undue respect for law is, that you may see a file of soldiers . . . marching in admirable order over hill and dale to the wars, against their wills, ay, against their common sense and consciences, which makes it very steep marching indeed. . . .

Many members and leaders of churches spoke out against the war. As the months passed, other voices joined in. Newspaperman Horace Greeley wrote in the *New York Tribune* that the war was unnecessary. Antislavery activist Frederick Douglass, who had once been a slave, called the war "disgraceful" and "cruel." The antislavery paper *The Liberator* went even further, wishing "the most triumphant success" to the Mexicans.

TEXAN MOUNTED MILITIA.

What about ordinary people? It's impossible to know how many of them supported the war, but there is evidence that some workers were against it. Many Irish workers showed up at an antiwar meeting in New York City. They called the war a plot by slave owners. The New England Workingmen's Association also spoke out against the war.

The flood of army volunteers slowed down after the first rush of excitement. To get enough soldiers, the army was forced to pay for new recruits. It also offered land to volunteers if they served for the entire war.

Some of the men who did enlist were shocked by the bloody horror of war. After a battle outside Matamoros, for example, fifty Americans and five hundred Mexicans lay dead or wounded on the field. The screaming and groaning from both sides was terrible to hear. Other new soldiers sickened and died in miserable, unhealthy conditions, such as the crowded ships that carried them to the front. And still others deserted to the Mexican side for better pay.

*(left)*
Texas Rangers, 1842.

## The Conquest of California

A SEPARATE WAR WENT ON IN CALIFORNIA. Soldiers moved into California by land and sea. One of them was a young naval officer who imagined what would happen when the United States owned this western territory. "Population will flow into the fertile regions of California," he wrote in his diary.

Americans in California raided Mexican settlements that had been founded by the Spanish. They stole horses. And they declared the territory independent, calling it the "Bear Flag Republic."

An American naval officer gathered chiefs from the Indian tribes in California and told them:

> The country you inhabit no longer belongs to Mexico, but to a mighty nation whose territory extends from the great ocean you have all seen or heard of [the Pacific], to another great ocean thousands of miles toward the rising sun [the Atlantic]. . . . Our armies are now in Mexico, and will soon conquer the whole country. But you have nothing to fear from us, if you do what is right . . . if you are faithful to your new rulers. . . . We shall watch over you and give you true liberty; but beware of sedition [treason], lawlessness, and all other crimes, for the army which shields can

assuredly punish, and it will reach you in your most
retired hiding places.

Meanwhile, American soldiers advanced westward through New Mexico. They captured the city
of Santa Fe without a battle. A few months later,
though, Mexicans in the nearby city of Taos
revolted against American rule. The revolt was
stopped, but some of the rebels escaped to the
hills. They carried out occasional attacks, killing
Americans, until the U.S. Army killed 150 of them
in a final battle.

In Los Angeles, too, there was a revolt.
Mexicans forced the American troops to surrender
in September 1846. The U.S. military did not
recapture Los Angeles until December, after a
bloody battle.

## Victory over Mexico

BY THIS TIME GENERAL TAYLOR HAD MOVED
across the Rio Grande and taken Matamoros. His
army was marching southward through Mexico.

The men were becoming hard to control. Soldiers got drunk and looted Mexican villages. Cases of rape increased.

At the same time, sickness and heat were killing the soldiers. A thousand of them died on the march. At Monterrey they fought another battle with the Mexicans. So many men and horses died in agony that one U.S. officer said that the ground was slippery with foam and blood.

The U.S. Navy fired shells on the Mexican coastal city of Veracruz, killing many civilians. One shell hit a post office. Another hit a hospital. After two days and 1300 shells, the city surrendered. An American reporter wrote, "The Mexicans variously estimate their losses at from 500 to 1000 killed and wounded, but all agree that the loss among the soldiery is comparatively small and the destruction among the women and children is very great."

General Winfield Scott now moved an army of ten thousand soldiers into the heart of Mexico. A series of battles that had little point killed thousands of people on both sides. Finally, the armies of the two nations met to fight for control of Mexico City. A Mexican merchant wrote to a friend about the American conquest of the city, "In some cases whole blocks were destroyed and a great number of men, women and children killed and wounded."

In spite of their victories, the American soldiers were getting tired of marching, fighting, and risking death. Desertions were a problem. In March 1847 the army reported over a thousand deserters. More than nine thousand deserted over the course of the war.

In northern Mexico, volunteers from Virginia, Mississippi, and North Carolina rebelled against their commander. He killed one of the mutineers, but two of his lieutenants refused to help him stop the mutiny. The army later forgave the rebellious soldiers in order to keep the peace.

The glory of victory was for the president and the generals, not for the deserters, the dead, and the wounded. Many men felt anger toward those who had led them into deadly conditions and battles where so many had died. One group, the Massachusetts Volunteers, had started with 630 men. They came home with three hundred dead, mostly from disease. At a celebration dinner on their return, the men hissed at their commander.

Some volunteers who made it home ended up with little to show for their soldiering. The government had promised them land, but speculators immediately showed up to buy the land from them. Many of the men, desperate for money, sold their 160 acres for less than fifty dollars.

When Mexico surrendered, some Americans thought that the United States should take the whole country. Instead, it took just half.

In February 1848 Mexico and the United States signed the Treaty of Guadalupe Hidalgo. In the treaty, Mexico gave the entire Southwest and California to the United States. It also agreed that the border between the two nations was the Rio Grande. The United States, in turn, agreed to pay Mexico $15 million. This let people say that the nation's new territories were bought, not seized by force. One American newspaper claimed that "we take nothing by conquest. . . . Thank God."

# CHAPTER NINE

# SLAVERY
# AND EMANCIPATION

THE UNITED STATES GOVERNMENT SUPPORTED
slavery because the economy of the South depended
upon it. As that economy grew, so did the number
of slaves. Between 1790 and 1860, the amount of
cotton that the South produced rose from one thousand tons a year to 1 million tons a year. In that
same period, the number of slaves rose from half a
million to 4 million. Slavery was so well established
that only something enormous—something like a
full-scale war—could end it.

## Slavery in the American South

THE UNITED STATES GOVERNMENT MADE
it illegal to import new slaves in 1808. Previously,
many northern port cities had benefited from the
slave trade. From 1808 on, slavery in the U.S. was
supposed to be limited to Africans who were
already enslaved and their children. But the
demand for new slaves was great, so the law was
often broken. In his book *From Slavery to Freedom*,
historian John Hope Franklin estimates that a
quarter of a million slaves were illegally imported
before the Civil War began in 1861.

How can slavery be described? Maybe only people who have experienced it can say what it was
like. People like John Little, a former slave, who
wrote:

> They say that slaves are happy, because they laugh, and
> are merry. I myself and three or four others, have
> received two hundred lashes in the day, and had our
> feet in fetters; yet, at night, we would sing and dance,
> and make others laugh at the rattling of our chains.
> Happy men we must have been! We did it to keep
> down trouble, and to keep our hearts from being com-
> pletely broken: that is as true as the gospel!

Desperation drove some slaves to revolt.

Probably the largest revolt in the United States took place near New Orleans in 1811. It involved four to five hundred slaves. The U.S. Army and militia forces attacked them and ended their revolt. In 1822 a free black man named Denmark Vesey tried to launch a revolt in South Carolina, but authorities found out about it and hanged him, along with thirty-four others. Then, in Virginia, in the summer of 1831, a slave named Nat Turner led about seventy others on a rampage from plantation to plantation. They murdered at least fifty-five men, women, and children. As their ammunition ran out, they were captured. Turner and others were hanged.

Other slaves ran away. Each year during the 1850s, about a thousand slaves escaped into the North, Canada, and Mexico. One famous escaped slave, Harriet Tubman, made nineteen dangerous trips back into slave territory, helping slaves escape on the Underground Railroad. She told them, "You'll be free or die."

Whites sometimes helped slaves, and that worried the authorities. Some feared that poor whites would encourage slave revolts—not just because they felt sorry for the slaves, but because they

hated the rich planters and wanted to see their property destroyed. Fanny Kemble, a famous actress who married a Southern planter, wrote in her journal that black slaves and white Irish workers were kept apart when they were building a canal in Georgia. The Irish were a "warm-hearted, generous people," she said, who "might actually take to sympathy with the slaves."

## The Abolition Movement

SOME WHITE AMERICANS DID "TAKE TO sympathy with the slaves." They were called abolitionists because they called for the abolition, or end, of slavery. They bravely wrote newspaper articles and made speeches against slavery. They also helped many slaves escape on the Underground Railroad, a network of people who worked together to conduct runaway slaves to free territory, providing "safe houses" for them along the way. But black abolitionists were the backbone of the movement against slavery.

*(left)*
Underground Railroad, 1893.

The North had about 130,000 free blacks in 1830. Twenty years later there were 200,000. Many of them worked to free those who remained enslaved in the South. One of them was David Walker, son of a slave, who sold old clothes in Boston. He wrote a pamphlet called *Walker's Appeal,* urging blacks to fight for their freedom:

> Let our enemies go on with their butcheries, and at once fill up their cup. Never make an attampt to gain our freedom or natural right . . . until you can see your way clear— when that hour arrives and you move, be not afraid or dismayed. . . . God has been pleased to give us two eyes, two hands, two feet and some sense in our heads as well as [the whites]. They have no more right to hold us in slavery than we have to hold them. . . . "Every dog must have its day," the American's is coming to its end.

The *Appeal* made southern slaveholders so angry that one of them offered a reward for David Walker's murder or capture. One summer day in 1830 Walker was found dead near the doorway of his shop.

Frederick Douglass was born into slavery, learned to read and write, and escaped into the North at the age of twenty-one. He became the most famous black man of his time, speaking and writing against slavery. Douglass called "the idea of being a free man some day" a dream that "all the powers of slavery" could not destroy.

After the war with Mexico, the U.S. government brought California and other new territories into the Union as nonslave states. In return, the government had to do something for the slave states, so it passed the Fugitive Slave Act of 1850. This law made it easy for slave owners to recapture runaway slaves even after they had fled to the Northern states. It made it easy for slave owners to just pick up free blacks they claimed had run away.

Northern abolitionists, black and white, fought against the act. The year after Congress passed the law, a runaway slave named Jerry was captured and put on trial. A crowd broke into the Syracuse, New York courthouse to set him free. On July 4, 1852, Frederick Douglass gave a speech that placed the shame of slavery on the whole nation, not just the South. He said:

Fellow Citizens: What to the American slave is your Fourth of July? I answer, a day that reveals to him more than all other days of the year, the gross injustice and cruelty to which he is the constant victim. . . .There is not a nation of the earth guilty of practices more shocking and bloody than are the people of these United States at this very hour.

The government of the United States did not strongly enforce the law that ended the slave trade, yet it enforced runaway slave laws. The government under President Andrew Jackson worked with the South to keep abolitionist newspapers from being mailed in Southern states. The nation's Supreme Court declared in 1857 that the slave Dred Scott, even though he had lived for some time in free territories, could not sue for his freedom because he was property, not a person.

That government would never accept an end to slavery through rebellion. Slavery would end only under conditions controlled by whites, and only when it suited the business and political needs of the North. Abraham Lincoln was the perfect figure to bring about the end of slavery.

Lincoln understood the needs of business. He shared the political ambition of the new Republican political party. Finally, he spoke the language of doing good, and he could argue with passion against slavery on moral grounds. At the same time, he acted with caution in the world of politics, and he feared that abolition would cause new problems. Although Lincoln believed that slavery was unjust, he could not see blacks as the equals of whites. The best thing to do, he thought, would be to free the slaves and send them back to Africa.

## The Civil War and Slavery

THE NORTHERN ELITE, THE BANKERS AND businessmen who directed the economy of the North, wanted their kind of economy to expand. They wanted free land, free labor, and taxes that favored manufacturers. Lincoln shared their ideas. Southern planters, on the other hand, felt that Lincoln and the Republicans would make their own pleasant, prosperous way of life impossible. So when Lincoln was elected president in the fall of 1860, seven Southern states seceded, or left the Union. When Lincoln tried to take back the federal base at Fort Sumter, North Carolina, by force, four more states seceded. The South formed the Confederacy, and the Civil War was on.

Abolitionists urged Lincoln to emancipate, or free, the slaves in the South. But Lincoln made it clear that he had not gone to war to free the slaves—his goal was to bring the South back into the Union. In a letter to abolitionist and newspaperman Horace Greeley, Lincoln wrote:

> My paramount object in this struggle is to save the Union, and it is not either to save or destroy Slavery. If I could save the Union without freeing any slave, I would do it; and if I could save it by freeing all the slaves, I would do it.

But as the war grew more bitter and the North grew more desperate to win, Lincoln began to act against slavery. In September 1862 he gave the southern states four months to stop fighting, warning that he would free their slaves if they did not come over to the Union side. The fighting continued. On January 1, 1863, Lincoln issued the Emancipation Proclamation, freeing slaves in areas that were fighting against the Union. Two years later, before the war ended, Congress passed the Thirteenth Amendment to the Constitution, which ended all slavery in the United States.

These changes affected African Americans in many ways—not all of them good. Once blacks were free to enter the Union army, the war started to look more like a war for black liberation. The more whites suffered, the more they resented blacks. Angriest of all were poor whites who were drafted into the army. Rich people could buy their way out of the draft for $300. That was a huge amount of money. At that time the average skilled worker (such as a carpenter) earned about two dollars a day. Unskilled workers earned less. Draft riots in 1863 in northern cities turned whites against their black neighbors in a wave of violence and death. And the treatment of black soldiers in the army and the northern cities showed that freedom might not bring acceptance or true equality. Black soldiers were given the dirtiest and hardest work, and when they were off duty whites sometimes attacked them on the street.

The Civil War was one of the bloodiest conflicts in history up to that time. It killed 600,000 people, out of a population of 30 million. By late 1864, the South was losing. Soldiers were in short supply—but there were 4 million slaves. When some Confederate leaders spoke of enlisting slaves, one

Heroes of the Colored
Race Lithograph, 1881.

shocked general wrote, "If slaves will make good soldiers, our whole theory of slavery is wrong." In March 1865 Jefferson Davis, president of the Confederacy, signed a law that let blacks serve in the army of the South. But before the law had any effect, the war ended. The South had lost, and its slaves learned that they were now free.

## Emancipation without Freedom

MANY YEARS AFTER THE WAR, AFRICAN Americans who had been young children in 1865 recalled the tears, songs, and hope of the slaves who heard the news of their emancipation. It was a time of great celebration, the dawn of a new day. Yet many blacks knew that their status after the war would not depend on a law that made them free. It would depend on whether they owned land or had to work for others.

Much land in the South either went back to the families of the Confederates or was bought by Northern land speculators and investors. Blacks could not afford to buy much of it. Ex-slave Thomas Hall said, "Lincoln got the praise for freeing us, but did he do it?" Hall felt that Lincoln gave the slaves freedom but did not give them the chance to support themselves. Freed slaves still had to depend on whites for work and survival.

The United States government had fought the slave states not to end slavery but to keep control of the enormous territory, resources, and market of the South. Still, the end of slavery brought new forces into politics. One force was white people concerned with racial equality. Some of them came south to teach or work for the Freedmen's Bureau that the government set up to aid the freed slaves. A second force was blacks determined to make their freedom mean something. A third force was the Republican Party. It wanted to keep control over the national government, and the votes of Southern blacks could help. Northern businessmen felt that Republican plans benefited them, so they went along for a while.

These forces created a brief period after the Civil War when blacks in the South voted, elected blacks to state legislatures and to the U.S. Senate and House of Representatives, and introduced free, racially mixed education. New laws protected them from discrimination and guaranteed them equal rights. But because blacks depended on whites for work, their votes could be bought or taken away by the threat of violence.

White violence against blacks erupted in the South almost as soon as the war ended. In May 1866, in Memphis, Tennessee, whites killed forty-six African Americans and burned more than a hundred homes, churches, and schools. The violence continued as white terrorist groups like the Ku Klux Klan organized raids, beatings, and racial murders called lynchings. The state of Kentucky alone had 116 acts of racial violence between 1867 and 1871.

As white violence rose in the 1870s, the national government grew less committed to protecting blacks. Northern politicians started to weigh the advantage of black voters' support against the advantage of a stable South controlled by whites who would accept Republican leadership. It was only a matter of time before blacks would be returned to a condition that was not far from slavery, even if they remained legally free.

In 1877 the Republican Party leaders made a deal to get their candidate, Rutherford Hayes, elected president. In return for the necessary electoral votes, they agreed to remove Union troops from the South. This took away the last military protection for southern blacks. Their legal protection was crumbling, too, as the Southern states passed laws that chipped away at equality. By the end of the nineteenth century, the U.S. Supreme Court approved laws that allowed segregation, or separation of people by race. Only one Supreme Court justice, a former slave owner named John Harlan, argued against segregation, saying, "Our Constitution is color-blind. . . ."

With its economy in ruins, the South needed money. A new alliance formed between the Northern bankers and investors and the Southern elites. They talked about the "New South" of coal and iron mines, business and railroads. The former slaves were swept out of the picture. By 1900, all of the southern states had passed laws that kept African Americans from voting and from enjoying equal rights.

At this low point for black people in America, blacks knew that they had been betrayed. Some fled the South, hoping to escape violence and poverty. Those who remained organized for self-defense, in the face of more than a hundred lynchings a year. Thomas Fortune, a young black editor for the *New York Globe,* told the Senate, "The white man who shoots a negro always goes free, while the negro who steals a hog is sent to the chain-gang for ten years."

W. E. B. Du Bois, a black man who came to teach at Atlanta University, saw the betrayal of the African Americans as part of something bigger that was happening in the United States. He said that poor whites and blacks were both being exploited, or used, by politicians and big business. Because whites could vote, they didn't think they were exploited. Du Bois said, though, that the "dictatorship of vast capital" limited the power of their votes. He was talking about the economic system called capitalism, in which private individuals or companies, rather than the state, own the farms and factories, set prices and compete with each other in the marketplace, and accumulate wealth.

Was Du Bois right? Did the growth of American capitalism mean that whites as well as blacks were in some sense becoming slaves?

# CHAPTER TEN

# THE OTHER CIVIL WAR

THE WAR BETWEEN NORTH AND SOUTH was not the only conflict in the United States during the nineteenth century. There was another war going on—a struggle between classes. This struggle is often left out of textbooks. Instead, textbooks can make it seem as though the history of the time was a clash between the Republican and Democratic political parties, even though both parties represented the classes that held most of the power in the country.

## The Myth of "Jacksonian Democracy"

ANDREW JACKSON, WHO WAS ELECTED
president in 1828, said he spoke for "the humble
members of society"—for workers and farmers.
He certainly did not speak for the Indians being
pushed off their lands or for enslaved African
Americans. But the government needed a large
base of support among white people, and the
myth of "Jacksonian Democracy" was designed to
win that support.

That myth led ordinary people to believe that
they had a voice in government and that government looked out for their interests. It was a way of
speaking for the lower and middle classes to get
their support when the government needed it.
Giving people a choice between two political parties, and letting them choose the slightly more
democratic one, was a good way to control them.
The leaders of both parties understood that they
could keep control of society by making reforms
that gave people some of what they wanted—but
not too much.

The United States was developing with enormous speed and excitement. It was turning into
an urban, or city-dwelling, nation. In 1790, fewer

than a million Americans lived in cities. By 1840, the figure was 11 million. New York City alone grew from 130,000 people in 1820 to a million in 1860.

Many city-dwellers lived in extreme poverty. Working-class families in Philadelphia crowded into apartment buildings called tenements, one family to a room, with no fresh water or toilets. In New York the poor lay in the streets with the garbage. The slums had no sewers. Filthy water drained into them, causing outbreaks of deadly diseases.

The very poor could not be counted on to support the government. They were like the slaves and Indians—invisible most of the time, but frightening to the elite if they started an uprising. Other citizens, though, might support the system. Farmers who owned their land, better-paid laborers, and urban office workers were paid just enough, and flattered just enough, that in a crisis they would be loyal to the system and the upper classes that dominated it.

## Big Business

BUSINESS WAS BOOMING IN NINETEENTH-century America. The opening of the West was helped by canals, railroads, and the telegraph. New equipment such as iron plows and mechanical reapers made farming more productive. But the economy was not planned or managed to meet human needs. Instead, it was driven by the quest for private profits. It cycled between booms (times of growth and prosperity) and slumps (times of depression and unemployment).

To make business more stable and to reduce competition, companies joined together. For example, many railroads merged to form one, the New York Central line. Companies also controlled competition by agreeing among themselves on the prices they would charge the public for their goods and services. In addition, they got help from the government. During just seven years in the 1850s, the state and federal governments gave away 25 million acres to railroad companies, along with millions of dollars in loans.

On the eve of the Civil War, the men who ran the country were most concerned with money and profit, not the movement against slavery.

A preacher named Theodore Parker told his congregation, "Money is this day the strongest power of the nation."

But the effort to keep politics and the economy under control did not quite work. From time to time, poor people showed their anger at the crowded cities, long hours in factories operating new industrial machines, high prices, lost jobs, disease, and miserable tenements. In 1827, as a meeting of mechanics (crafts and trades workers), one young man spoke of how hard it was to make a living, and of how laborers were at the mercy of their bosses:

> We find ourselves oppressed on every hand—we labor hard in producing all the comforts of life for the enjoyment of others, while we ourselves obtain but a scanty portion, and even that in the present state of society depends on the will of employers.

Sometimes there were sudden, unorganized uprisings against the rich. Sometimes the anger got turned against blacks, Catholics, or immigrants. And sometimes the poor organized their anger into demonstrations and strikes against the bankers, land speculators, landlords, and merchants who controlled the economy.

## Workers Unite

IN 1829, THE WORKING PEOPLE OF
Philadelphia held one of the first citywide meetings
of labor groups in the United States. Frances
Wright, a Scottish political thinker and women's
rights activist, was invited to speak. Wright asked if
the Revolutionary War had been fought "to crush
down the sons and daughters of your country's
industry." She wondered whether the new industrial machinery was lowering the value of human
labor, making people servants to the machines, and
crippling the minds and bodies of child laborers.

Trade unions began to form as workers banded
together to bargain for better pay and working
conditions. In 1835, workers in fifty different
trades, such as bookbinding and cabinetmaking,
organized labor unions in Philadelphia. They
refused to work until their workday was limited to
ten hours. Their strike succeeded.

The courts struck back at unions, calling them
illegal conspiracies to hurt business. After a New
York court ordered a "conspiracy" of tailors to pay
a fine, twenty-seven thousand people gathered in
front of City Hall to protest the court's decision. A
handbill was seen in the city:

*(left)*
Construction crew
with wood burning
balloon-stack locomotive
at a crossing of the
Green River, 1885.

THE RICH AGAINST THE POOR!

Mechanics and working men! A deadly blow has been
struck at your liberty! . . . They have established . . .
that workingmen have no right to regulate the price of
labor, or, in other words, the rich are the only judges
of the wants of the poor man.

Later, farmers and working people across New
York State formed the Equal Rights Party to run
their own candidates for political office.

An economic crisis in 1837 caused prices of
food, fuel, and rent to soar. In New York City, a
third of the working class, or about fifty thousand
people, had no jobs. The Equal Rights Party organized a giant rally that turned into a riot when the
crowd stormed a store full of flour and wheat.

The labor movement had started off well in
Philadelphia. When religious conflict developed
between American-born Protestant workers in the
weaving trade and Irish immigrant Catholic
weavers, however, the movement fell apart.

The Irish were fleeing starvation in their own
country, where a plant disease had killed the potato
crop. These new immigrants, poor and discriminated against, had little sympathy for the plight of
black slaves in the United States. Most working-class

activists, in fact, ignored the African Americans.
Ely Moore, a New York trade union leader who
was elected to Congress, argued against abolition.
Racism was an easy substitute for the true frustra-
tion of the working classes against the upper classes.

In 1850 the United States had a workforce of
about 8.25 million people. Most of these people,
free or slave, still worked in agriculture. A half
million women worked outside their homes. The
majority of them worked as servants. Others
worked in factories (especially mills that made tex-
tiles, or cloth). About 55,000 were teachers.

Women textile workers were very active in the
labor movement. Girls and women who worked in
the mills of Lowell, Massachusetts, repeatedly
struck for better conditions. One strike, for example, was for a workday of eleven hours rather than
thirteen and a half hours. Another strike inspired
an eleven-year-old protestor named Harriet
Hanson to join the strikers:

> [W]hen the girls in my room stood irresolute [undecided],
> uncertain what to do . . . I, who began to think they would
> not go out, after all their talk, became impatient, and
> started on ahead, saying, with childish bravado, "I don't
> care what you do, I am going to turn out, whether anyone

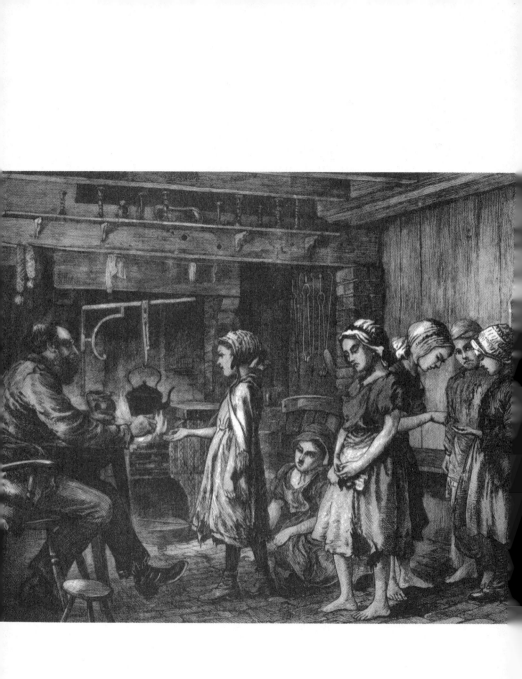

else does or not," and I marched out, and was followed by the others. As I looked back at the long line that followed me, I was more proud than I have ever been since. . . .

Children started the first mill strike in Paterson, New Jersey. When the company changed their meal hour from noon to 1, the children marched off the job. Their parents cheered them on. Other working people joined the strike, which became a ten-day struggle.

Shoemakers in Lynn, Massachusetts, suffered during an economic depression in 1857. Many lost their jobs. Others had their wages cut. The shoe-makers started a strike that spread to twenty-five towns and lasted for several months. Eventually, the factory owners offered higher wages to bring the workers back, but they refused to recognize the unions. Workers still had to face their employ-ers as individuals.

During the Civil War, workers in the North had to pay high prices for food and other necessities of life, while their wages were kept low. There were strikes all over the country. In 1863, a newspaper printed a list of strikes, protests, and labor actions under the headline "Revolution in New York." The hidden anger of the poor was coming out.

*(left)*
Paying children for their labor in the brickyards, 1871.

White workers of the North were not enthusiastic about a war that seemed to be fought for the black slave or for the capitalist. The war, they thought, was bringing profit to a new class of millionaires. Some of their strikes ended under the threat of force by troops from the Union army.

Another source of conflict was the drafting of soldiers into the Union army. Men rich enough to pay $300 could get out of serving. The poor had no choice to but risk death on the battlefield. Draft riots broke out in New York and other cities. Poor people and workers raged against many targets: the rich, the blacks, and the Republicans. Mobs destroyed factories and the homes of wealthy people. They also burned a black orphanage and killed African Americans in the street. Troops had to be brought in to restore order.

The South had its own class conflict. Millions of Southern whites were poor farmers who did not own slaves. Some of them lived little better than slaves. Just as in the North, the poor were drafted into the army while the rich could buy their way out, and just as in the North, draft riots erupted.

## Rule and Rebellion

UNDER THE NOISE OF WAR, CONGRESS and Lincoln made a series of laws that gave business what it wanted. The Morrill Tariff made foreign goods more expensive. This let American manufacturers raise their own prices so that consumers had to pay more for goods. The Contract Labor Law let employers bring in foreign workers who would work in exchange for their passage to the United States. This gave business a source of cheap labor and of strikebreakers—people to take the jobs of unionized workers who went on strike. Laws gave mill owners the right to flood other people's property, and other laws gave farmers' land to railroad and canal companies.

State and federal laws did not even pretend to protect working people. There were almost no health and safety laws. The laws that did exist were not enforced. When a mill collapsed, killing eighty-eight workers, the court found the owners free of blame, even though there was evidence that they knew the building could not support the heavy machinery inside.

After the war, soldiers returned, looking for work. They found that women had joined the industrial workforce during the war. Moving beyond the textile mills and tailoring jobs, women had become cigar makers and printers. Some of them had their own unions. Black workers, too, formed unions of their own.

Another economic crisis struck the country in 1873. It was one of a string of depressions that wiped out small businesses and brought hunger, cold, and death to working people while the rich remained secure—or grew richer.

The depression continued through the 1870s. Tens of thousands of people lost their jobs, even their homes. Many roamed the countryside, looking for food. Desperate people tried to get to Europe or South America. Unemployed workers held mass meetings to demand relief from the government.

In 1877, with the country in the depths of the depression, a series of railroad strikes shook the nation. Railroad workers in Martinsburg, West Virginia, went on strike to protest wage cuts and dangerous work conditions that led to deaths and injuries. They halted train traffic. Federal troops got the trains moving again, but in Baltimore citizens who supported the strikers surrounded the National Guard armory, hurling rocks at soldiers.

The soldiers answered with bullets, killing ten men and boys. A battle raged at the train depot, where the crowd smashed up an engine.

The rebellion of the railroad workers spread to Pittsburgh. After troops there killed ten people, the whole city rose in anger. Thousands looted the freight cars. Fires and fighting enveloped the city. Strikes and riots followed in Reading, Pennsylvania, and in Chicago, St. Louis, and New York. The authorities responded swiftly and violently.

When a crowd of young people shut down Chicago's railroads, lumberyards, and mills, calling workers to strike, the police attacked. "The sound of clubs falling on skulls was sickening for the first minute, until one grew used to it," said a newspaper article. "A rioter dropped at every whack, it seemed, for the ground was covered with them." At a peaceful labor meeting in New York, the speaker declared, "Whatever we poor men may not have, we have free speech, and no one can take it from us." Then the police charged, using their clubs.

The great railroad strikes of 1877 halted more than half the freight on the nation's rail lines.

When they were over, a hundred people were dead, and a thousand had gone to jail, a hundred thousand workers had gone on strike, and countless other unemployed people in the cities had been roused into action.

The railroads gave workers a few benefits. They also strengthened their own police forces. Nothing had really changed. Just as African Americans had learned that they did not have enough strength to make good the promises of emancipation, working people learned that they were not united or strong enough to defeat the combination of private wealth and government power. But their fight would continue.

# CHAPTER ELEVEN

# ROBBER BARONS
# AND REBELS

BETWEEN THE CIVIL WAR AND 1900, STEAM
and electricity replaced human muscle. The
United States built 193,000 miles of railroads.
New tools such as the telegraph, telephone, and
typewriter speeded up the work of business. Oil
and coal drove the machinery of factories and
lighted the streets and homes of cities. Inventors
and businesspeople made all this happen.

Some inventors were also businessmen.
Thomas Edison didn't just invent electrical equipment, he marketed it as well. Other businessmen
built corporations and fortunes by putting together
other people's inventions. A Chicago butcher
named Gustavus Swift combined the ice-cooled railway car with the ice-cooled warehouse to start the
country's first meat-packing plant in 1885.

Progress demanded labor. Much of the work was done by immigrants, who poured into the United States faster than ever before—5.5 million in the 1880s, 4 million in the 1890s. Many of those who came to the East Coast were from southern and eastern Europe. On the West Coast, Chinese immigrants made up one-tenth of California's population in 1880. Chinese and Jewish newcomers became the targets of racial attacks, sometimes at the hands of those who had immigrated earlier, such as the Irish.

Violence against immigrants could be murderous. In Rock Springs, Wyoming, in 1885, whites killed twenty-eight Chinese immigrants. Earlier, author Bret Harte wrote these words in memory of Wan Lee, a Chinese man killed in California:

> Dead, my revered friends, dead. Stoned to death in the
> streets of San Francisco, in the year of grace 1869 by a
> mob of halfgrown boys and Christian schoolchildren.

The greatest march of economic growth in human history took place in the United States in the late nineteenth century. The wealth it produced was like a pyramid. The supporting layers, those who built the pyramid and held it up, were the workers: blacks, whites, Chinese and

*(left)*
Thomas Edison with dynamo that generated the first commercial electric light, 1890s.

European immigrants, women. At the top were the new American multimillionaires.

## The Rich Get Richer

SOME MULTIMILLIONAIRES STARTED IN poverty. Their "rags to riches" stories were useful for making the masses of poor workers believe that they, too, could be wealthy someday. The great majority of millionaires, however, came from upper-class or middle-class families. Those who went on to become the richest men of the era—J. P. Morgan, John D. Rockefeller, Andrew Carnegie, James Mellon, and Jay Gould—could afford to escape military service in the Civil War by paying substitutes to take their places. Mellon's father wrote to him, "There are plenty of lives less valuable [than yours]."

These men and others built huge fortunes with the help of the government and the courts. Sometimes they had to pay for that help. Thomas Edison, for example, promised New Jersey politicians

$1,000 each if they would make laws to favor his business interests.

History books often call the first transcontinental railroad a great American achievement. It was built on blood, sweat, politics, and thievery by two railway companies. The Central Pacific line started on the West Coast and went east. It spent $200,000 on bribes in Washington, D.C. to get free land and loans, and it paid its Irish and Chinese workers one or two dollars a day. The Union Pacific line started in Nebraska and went west. To avoid being investigated, it bribed congressmen by selling them shares in the company very cheaply. Its workers died by the hundreds from heat, cold, and attacks by Indians who fought the invasion of their land.

Rockefeller built a fortune in the new oil business, partly by making secret deals with railroad companies. He promised to ship his oil with them if they would give him lower rates. This arrangement saved him money, so he could sell his oil for less, which drove competing oil companies out of business. He bought them up and created a monopoly—a system in which one corporation controls all or most of an industry.

The efficient businessmen of the late nineteenth century are sometimes called robber barons. They were powerful, like the barons of medieval nobility, and much of their wealth was gained through greedy or dishonest methods. In industry after industry they created empires by keeping prices high and wages low, by crushing their competition, and by getting help from the government in the form of favorable laws and taxes. The government pretended to be neutral, but in reality it served the interests of the rich. Its purpose was to settle disputes among the upper classes peacefully, to keep the lower classes under control, and to keep the economic system stable.

The election of Grover Cleveland in 1884 showed the way things were in the United States. Many people thought that Cleveland, a Democrat, was against the power of monopolies and corporations. But Cleveland promised the captains of industry, "No harm shall come to any business interest . . . so long as I am President." After he was elected, Cleveland showed that he cared more about the rich than the poor. He refused to give $100,000 of federal money to help Texas farmers buy seed grain during a drought, even though the treasury was full of funds. That same year, Cleveland bought back government bonds held by wealthy people at more than their face value—a gift of $45 million to the rich.

## Voices of Protest

A FEW POLITICIANS TRIED TO LIMIT THE power of corporations. To break up monopolies, Senator John Sherman wrote the Sherman Anti-Trust Act, which Congress voted into law in 1877. Sherman feared that without reforms, people who opposed the power of giant corporations might be drawn to dangerous new political ideas that had come out of Europe.

One idea was socialism—an economic system in which the government or the people as a whole own the means of production, such as farms, mines, and factories. These are operated for the benefit of all, not for private profit. Communism went even further, doing away with private property and with class distinctions based on wealth. In a

communist society, all goods would be owned by everyone, available to anyone according to need. A third new political idea, anarchism, held that government itself was unnecessary, even wrong.

The Sherman Anti-Trust Act was designed to reform the capitalist system just enough to prevent socialism or communism from taking hold among the workers and poor. Less than twenty years after it became law, however, the U.S. Supreme Court interpreted the act in a way that made it meaningless. At the same time, the Court was giving added protection to corporations. These decisions kept wealth at the top of the pyramid. One Supreme Court justice, David J. Brewer, said in 1893, "It is the unvarying law that the wealth of the community will be in the hands of the few. . ."

Churches, schools, business, and government tried to control people's thinking, teaching them that all was right with society. Poverty was a sign of personal failure. The rich deserved to be rich. The capitalist system was right and proper.

Not everyone accepted that view of things. Some people were ready to consider harsh criticism of the system, or to imagine other ways of living. One of

*(left)* Illustration from *Harper's Weekly* depicting the Homestead Strike of 1892.

them was Henry George, a self-educated Philadelphia workingman who became a newspaperman and economist. People around the world read his 1879 book *Progress and Poverty.* George argued that a tax on land, which he called the basis of wealth, would raise enough money that the government could solve the problem of poverty. Another writer, a lawyer named Edward Bellamy, published *Looking Backward,* a novel about life in the year 2000. In Bellamy's hopeful view of the future, society was socialistic. Everyone worked and lived in cooperation, not as competing individuals.

Great movements of workers and farmers swept the land in the 1880s and 1890s. These went beyond the scattered strikes of earlier years. They were national movements that threatened the ruling elites. Revolutionary societies existed in American cities, and revolutionary talk was in the air.

In 1883, an anarchist congress took place in Pittsburgh. It drew up a statement that called for "equal rights for all without distinction to sex or race." It quoted an 1848 document called the *Communist Manifesto,* which declared, "Workmen of all lands, unite! You have nothing to lose but your chains; you have a world to win!"

## The Haymarket Affair

IN 1886, THE EXISTING SYSTEM AND
the new ideas clashed. The American Federation
of Labor, a five-year-old association of labor
unions, called for nationwide strikes wherever
employers refused to shorten the workday to eight
hours. About 350,000 employees of more than
11,500 businesses went out on strike.

In Chicago alone, forty thousand people struck
(another 45,000 received a shorter workday to
keep them from striking). Outside one factory,
workers and their supporters got into a fight with
*scabs*—their term for the workers who stepped in
to do their jobs while they were on strike. Police
fired into the crowd, killing four strikers. After
that, August Spies, an anarchist and labor leader,
published a sheet telling workers to take up arms
against the bosses. Other anarchists spoke at a
mass meeting at Haymarket Square, to an audi-
ence of about four thousand people. It was a
peaceful meeting. Still, police arrived and ordered
the crowd to leave. Just then, a bomb exploded,
wounding sixty-six policemen. Seven of them
died. The police fired, wounding two hundred
people and killing several.

No evidence was found to show who had thrown the bomb. The authorities arrested Spies and seven other anarchists on the charge that they had urged murder. Under Illinois law, that was the same as committing murder. The evidence against the eight was their ideas and their literature, not their actions. Only one of them had been at Haymarket Square. But a jury found all eight guilty, and seven were sentenced to death. (Four were hanged, one killed himself before he could be executed, and the other three were eventually pardoned and released.)

People around the world demonstrated against the harsh sentences. In Chicago, twenty-five thousand marched in protest. Year after year, all over the country, memorial meetings for the Haymarket martyrs took place. Some people were shocked into political action by the Haymarket Affair.

## The Rise and Fall of Populism

THE HAYMARKET EXECUTIONS DID NOT crush the labor movement. The year 1886 became known as "the year of the great uprising of labor." Unions formed in the sugar fields of the South, and workers went on strike. After two black strike leaders in Louisiana were arrested and then disappeared never to be seen again, gun battles broke out between strikers and militia. An African American newspaper in New Orleans reported on the violence in the town of Thibodaux:

> Lame men and blind women shot; children and hoary-headed grandsires ruthlessly swept down! The Negroes offered no resistance; they could not, as the killing was unexpected. Those of them not killed took to the woods . . . Citizens of the United States killed by a mob directed by a State judge. . . . Laboring men seeking an advance in wages, treated as if they were dogs!

A few years later, coal miners struck in Tennessee. When mine owners sent in convicts to do the work, the miners took over the mine by force. Workers at Andrew Carnegie's steel plant in Homestead, Pennsylvania, also struck. The governor sent militia to control the strike, and the plant used strikebreakers to keep producing steel. After two months, the strike collapsed.

In 1893, the country entered the biggest economic crisis it had seen. The depression lasted for years and brought a wave of strikes. A railroad workers' strike was the largest and most violent. It launched one worker, Eugene Debs, into a lifetime of activism for labor unions and socialism. Debs was arrested for supporting the strike. Two years later he wrote:

> The issue is Socialism versus Capitalism. I am for Socialism because I am for humanity. We have been cursed with the reign of gold long enough. Money constitutes no proper basis for civilization. The time has come to regenerate [renew] society—we are on the eve of a universal change.

Like laborers, farmers were suffering. The cost of things like farm machinery and railroad fees for shipping grain kept going up, but the prices for farm produce went down. Many farmers could not pay their bills, and they lost their farms.

Farmers began creating union-like organizations to help each other. They bought goods together to get lower prices, and they worked to get pro-farm laws passed. One of these associations, the Farmers

Alliance, gave birth to a new movement called populism (political and economic beliefs and activities "of the people"). It promoted the idea that farmers acting together could build their own institutions—such as affordable insurance against crop loss—and their own political parties.

In general, populists were against monopolies (also called trusts) and capitalism. They wanted the government to control railway rates and banks' interest rates, to keep them from making huge profits. Populists did not agree, however, on race. Some blacks and whites argued for racial unity, feeling that all poor agricultural workers were in the same fix and needed to stand together. Yet racism was strong in other white populists, while many more simply did not think that race was as important as the economic system. Many populists were also against new immigrants. They especially opposed immigration from eastern and southern Europe and from Asia.

In the end, the populist movement failed to unite blacks and whites, farmers and urban workers. A few candidates ran for political office under the banner of the Populist or People's party, but in city after city populists allied themselves with the

Democratic party to have a better chance of winning elections. But it was political deal-makers, not revolutionary farmers, who won most elections. Eventually, the populist movement was lost in the sea of Democratic politics.

In the 1896 election, the corporations and press threw their support behind the Republican candidate, William McKinley. It was the first campaign in which massive amounts of money were spent, and McKinley was the winner. Like many politicians, he turned to patriotism to drown out class resentment. "I am glad to know that the people in every part of this country mean to be devoted to one flag, the glorious Stars and Stripes," he said. Then McKinley showed that he thought that money was as important, as sacred, as patriotism. He added, "the people of this country mean to maintain the financial honor of this country as sacredly as they maintain the honor of the flag."

# CHAPTER TWELVE
# THE AMERICAN EMPIRE

"I SHOULD WELCOME ALMOST ANY WAR, for I think this country needs one." Those words were written in 1897, in a letter to a friend, by Theodore Roosevelt, who would later become president of the United States. Why would he think that the nation needed a war?

Maybe a war would take up some of the rebellious energy that people were pouring into strikes and protests. Maybe it would unite the people with the armed forces against a foreign enemy. And there was another reason—an economic one.

Before he was elected president, William McKinley had said, "We want a foreign market for our surplus goods." Senator Albert Beveridge of Indiana spelled it out in 1897. He said:

American factories are making more than the American people can use; American soil is producing more than they can consume. Fate has written our policy for us; the trade of the world must and shall be ours.

These politicians and others believed that the United States had to open up other countries to American goods—even if those markets were not eager to buy. If factories and farms could sell their surplus production overseas, American companies would keep earning money, and the economy might avoid the crises that had sparked class war in the 1890s.

War was probably not a thought-out plan among most of the elite ruling classes. Instead, it grew naturally from two sources, capitalism and nationalism. Capitalism demanded more markets. Nationalism, the spirit of strong national pride, made people think that the United States had a right, or even a duty, to expand itself and to shape the affairs of other countries.

## The Taste of Empire

STRETCHING THE UNITED STATES' ARM
overseas was not a new idea. The war against
Mexico had already carried the United States to
the Pacific Ocean. Before that, in 1823, President
James Monroe had produced the Monroe
Doctrine. This statement made it clear that the
United States claimed an interest in the politics of
the entire Western Hemisphere—North, Central,
and South America. It warned the nations of
Europe not to meddle with countries in the
Americas.

The United States, however, didn't feel that it
had to stay out of other countries' affairs. Between
1798 and 1895, the United States sent troops to
other countries, or took an active role in their
affairs, 103 times. In the 1850s, for example, the
U.S. Navy used warships to force Japan to open its
ports to American shipping.

At the end of the nineteenth century, many
military men, politicians, and businessmen supported the idea of still more foreign involvement.
A writer for the *Washington Post* said:

> A new consciousness seems to have come upon us—the
> consciousness of strength—and with it a new appetite, the

yearning to show our strength. . . . The taste of Empire is
in the mouth of the people. . . .

## The Spanish-American War

THE AMERICAN PEOPLE MIGHT BE MORE
willing to enter into an overseas conflict if it
looked like a good deed, such as helping a nation's
people overthrow foreign rule. Cuba, an island
close to Florida, was in that situation. For centuries Spain had held Cuba as a colony. Then, in
1895, the Cubans rebelled against Spanish rule.

Some Americans thought that the United
States should help the Cubans because they were
fighting for freedom, like the colonists in the
Revolutionary War. The U.S. government was
more interested in who would control Cuba if the
Spanish were thrown out.

Race was part of the picture, because Cuba
had both black and white people. The administration of President Grover Cleveland feared that a
victory by the Cuban rebels might lead to "a white

*(left)*
Cuban fighters
in the war for
independence from
Spain roast a pig
during a break in
the fighting, 1896.

183

and a black republic." A young British empire builder named Winston Churchill, son of an American mother, had the same thought. In 1896 he wrote a magazine article saying that even though Spanish rule in Cuba was bad, and the rebels had the support of the Cuban people, it would be better if Spain stayed in control. If the rebels won, Cuba might become "another black republic." Churchill was warning that Cuba might be like Haiti, the first country in the Americas to be run by black people.

As Americans debated about whether to join the war in Cuba, an explosion in the harbor of Havana, Cuba's capital, destroyed the U.S. battleship *Maine*. The ship had been sent to Cuba as a symbol of American interest in the region. No evidence was ever produced to show what caused the explosion, but the loss of the *Maine* moved President McKinley and the country in the direction of war. It was clear that the United States could not get Spain out of Cuba without a fight. It was also clear that the United States couldn't carve out American military and economic interests in Cuba without sending troops to the island.

In April 1898 McKinley asked Congress to

declare war. Soon American forces moved into Cuba. The Spanish-American War had begun.

John Hay, the U.S. secretary of state, later called it a "splendid little war." The Spanish forces were defeated in three months. Nearly 5,500 American soldiers died. Only 379 died in battle. The rest were killed by disease and other causes. One cause was certainly the tainted, rotten meat sold to the army by American meatpackers.

What about the Cuban rebels who had started the fight with Spain? The American military pretended that they did not exist. When the Spanish surrendered, no Cuban was allowed to discuss the surrender, or sign the treaty. The United States was in control. U.S. troops remained in Cuba after the surrender. Soon, U.S. money entered the island, as Americans started taking over railroads, mines, and sugar plantations.

The United States told the Cuban people that they could write their own constitution and form their own government. It also told them that the U.S. Army would not leave the island until Cuba's new constitution included a new American law called the Platt Amendment. This law gave the United States the right to involve itself in Cuba's

affairs pretty much whenever it wanted. General
Leonard Wood explained to Theodore Roosevelt in
1901, "There is, of course, little or no independence left Cuba under the Platt Amendment."

Many Americans felt that the Platt
Amendment betrayed the idea of Cuban independence. Criticism went beyond the radicals
(socialists and others with extreme or revolutionary views) to mainstream newspapers and civic
groups. One group critical of the Platt
Amendment was the Anti-Imperialism League.
One of the League's founders was William James,
a philosopher at Harvard University, who opposed
the United States' trend toward empire building
and meddling in other county's affairs. In the end,
though, the Cubans had no choice but to agree to
the Platt Amendment if they wanted to set up
their own government.

## Revolt and Racism in the Philippines

THE UNITED STATES DID NOT ANNEX CUBA,
or make it part of U.S. territory. But the Spanish-
American War did lead to annexation of some
other territories that Spain had controlled. One
was Puerto Rico, an island neighbor of Cuba. The
United States had already taken over the Hawaiian
Islands from its Hawaiian Queen, and the war
gave it control of some other Pacific islands, too:
Wake Island, Guam, and the large island cluster
called the Philippines.

Americans hotly debated whether or not they
should take over the Philippines. One story says that
President McKinley told a visiting group of ministers
how he had come to the decision to annex the
Philippines. As he prayed for guidance, he became
convinced that "there was nothing left for us to do but
to take them all and to educate the Filipinos, and uplift
and civilize and Christianize them. . . . And then I
went to bed and went to sleep and slept soundly."

The Filipinos, however, did not get a message
from God telling them to accept American rule.
Instead, in February 1899 they rose up in revolt
against the United States, just as they had revolted
several times against Spain.

The taste of empire was on the lips of politicians and businessmen throughout the United States, and they agreed that the United States must keep control of its new territory. Talk of money mingled with talk of destiny and civilization. "The Philippines are ours forever," Senator Beveridge told the U.S. Senate. "And just beyond the Philippines are China's illimitable markets [markets with no limits or boundaries]. We will not retreat from either."

It took the United States three years to crush the Filipino rebellion. It was a harsh war. Americans lost many more troops than in Cuba. For the Filipinos the death rate was enormous, from battle and from disease.

McKinley said that the fighting with the rebels started when the rebels attacked American forces. Later, American soldiers testified that the United States had fired the first shot.

The famous American author Mark Twain summed up the Philippine war with disgust, saying:

> We have pacified some thousands of the islanders and buried them; destroyed their fields; burned their villages, and turned their widows and orphans out-of-doors. . . . And so, by these Providences of God—the phrase is the government's, not mine—we are a World Power.

*(left)*
A long line of African American soldiers who fought in the Spanish-American War, 1899.

The Anti-Imperialist League worked to educate the American public about the horrors of the Philippine war and the evils of imperialism, or empire building. It published letters from soldiers on duty in the Philippines. There were reports of soldiers killing women, children, and prisoners of war. A black soldier named William Fulbright wrote from Manila, the capital of the Philippines, "This struggle on the islands has been naught but a gigantic scheme of robbery and oppression."

Race was an issue in the Philippines, as it had been in Cuba. Some white American soldiers were racists who considered the Filipinos inferior. Black American soldiers in the Philippines had mixed feelings. Some felt pride, the desire to show that blacks were as courageous and patriotic as whites. Some wanted the chance to get ahead in life through the military. But others felt that they were fighting a brutal war against people of color—not too different from the violence against black people in the United States, where drunken white soldiers in Tampa, Florida, started a race riot by using a black child for target practice.

Back in the United States, many African Americans turned against the Philippine war because they saw it as a racial conflict, the white race fighting to conquer the brown. They were fighting injustice at home, too. A group of African Americans in Massachusetts sent a message to President McKinley, criticizing him for doing nothing to advance racial equality.

Throughout the nineteenth century, black Americans, along with women, workers, and the poor, had raised their voices against oppression. Many had found ways to resist the harshest effects of a political and economic system that ignored them. In the coming century, they would take their own steps toward change.

# Glossary

**Abolitionism** Movement to abolish, or end, something, such as slavery

**Anarchism** A belief that governments are by nature oppressive, and that people should live free from the authority of the state, the church, and corporate power, and share the wealth of the earth

**Annex** To take control of a territory and add it to a country

**Capitalism** Economic system in which income-producing property (such as farms and factories) is owned by individuals or corporations and competititon in a free marketplace determines how goods and services will be distributed and priced

**Communism** The idea that capitalism has outlived its usefulness, that it must be replaced by a system in which the economy is collectively managed, and its wealth distributed according to people's needs

**Conservative** Tending to support established institutions and traditional values and to be wary of social change

**Democracy** Government that is ruled by the people, who usually elect representatives to form the government

**Depression** A period of low economic activity and high unemployment

**Elite** A group that is powerful within a society, often because of having money, or hereditary authority, or noble status

**Emigrant** Someone who leaves his or her home country to live in a different country

**Federalist** Supporter of a strong central, or federal, authority; supporter of national interests over states' rights

**Feminism** The belief that women are equal to men and deserve equal rights

**Immigrant** Someone who comes into a country to live there

**Imperialism** Empire building

**Indenture** A contract that binds a person to work for someone else for a certain length of time

**Left-wing** Liberal or radical

**Liberal** Tending to support strong civil liberties and to be open to social change

**Massacre** Killing a number of people, usually in a brutal or violent way

**Militia** Citizens who are armed and can act as soldiers in an emergency

**Monopoly** An economic situation in which an entire industry is controlled by a single corporation, or just a few of them

**Nationalism** Strong loyalty to one's country or ethnic group, with the feeling that that country or group is more important than others, or has higher standing, and that its interests should always be supported

**Racism** The belief that racial differences make some people better or worse than others; also, treating people differently because of race

**Radical** Extremely critical of the existing social system

**Ratification** The process by which something is voted on, accepted, and made into law

**Right-wing** Politically **conservative**

**Socialism** A society of equality, in which not profit but usefulness determines what is produced

**Speculator** Someone who buys large amounts of land, not to use it but to resell it at a profit

**Strike** An action by people in a **union** who refuse to work until their demands are met

**Suffrage** The right to vote

**Terrorism** Acts of violence, possibly against civilians, carried out for political reasons by people who do not formally represent a state or its armed forces

**Union** Association of workers who bargain for wages and benefits together instead of one by one

# Index

**HOWARD ZINN** is professor emeritus at Boston University. He is the author of the classic *A People's History of the United States*, "a brilliant and moving history of the American people from the point of view of those whose plight has been largely omitted from most histories" (Library Journal). The book has now sold more than one million copies.

Zinn has received the Lannan Foundation Literary Award for Nonfiction and the Eugene V. Debs award for his writing and political activism, and in 2003 was awarded the Prix des amis du Monde Diplomatique.

Zinn is the author of numerous books, including *A Power Governments Cannot Suppress, Voices of A People's History of the United States* (with Anthony Arnove), *The Zinn Reader*, the autobiographical *You Can't Be Neutral on a Moving Train*, and the play *Marx in Soho*.

Zinn grew up in Brooklyn and worked in the shipyards before serving as an air force bombardier in World War II. Zinn was chair of the History Department at Spelman College, where he actively participated in the Civil Rights Movement, before taking a position at Boston University. While there he became a leader in the movement to end the war in Vietnam.

He now lives with his wife, Roslyn, in Massachusetts and lectures widely on history, contemporary politics, and against war.

**REBECCA STEFOFF** is the author of many books for children and young adults. In addition to writing on a number of topics in American history, including a biography of the Shawnee chieftain Tecumseh and a ten-volume series of historical atlases, she has adapted Ronald Takaki's award-winning history of Asian Americans, *Strangers from a Different Shore,* into a series for young readers. Stefoff received her B.A. from Indiana University and her M.A. from the University of Pennsylvania. Currently she lives in Portland, Oregon.

*About the Publisher*

**SEVEN STORIES PRESS** is an independent book publisher based in New York City, with distribution throughout the United States, Canada, England, and Australia. We publish works of the imagination by such writers as Nelson Algren, Octavia E. Butler, Assia Djebar, Ariel Dorfman, Barry Gifford, Lee Stringer, and Kurt Vonnegut, to name a few, together with political titles by voices of conscience, including the Boston Women's Health Book Collective, Noam Chomsky, Ralph Nader, Gary Null, Project Censored, Barbara Seaman, Gary Webb, and Howard Zinn, among many others. Our books appear in hardcover, paperback, pamphlet, and e-book formats, in English and in Spanish. We believe publishers have a special responsibility to defend free speech and human rights, and to celebrate the gifts of the human imagination, wherever we can.

For more information about us, visit our Web site at www.sevenstories.com or write for a free catalogue to Seven Stories Press, 140 Watts Street, New York, NY 10013.